Absent from School
The story of a truancy centr

Rob Grunsell

After founding the Intermedia
whose story is told in this book
suspended pupils. This promp _____ _____ *Control?*, now
published in the Chameleon ser___

Absent from School

The story of a truancy centre

Rob Grunsell

Writers and Readers in association with **Chameleon**

First published as *Born to be Invisible* by Macmillan Education 1978
Published with the present title in 1980 by Writers and Readers
9—19 Rupert St, London W1V 7FS
in association with Chameleon
22 Bicester Road, Richmond, Surrey

Typeset by Shanta Thawani, 25 Natal Road, London N11 2HU
Printed and bound in Great Britain
by Whitstable Litho Ltd., Whitstable, Kent

case ISBN 0 906495 61 X
paper ISBN 0 906495 42 3

'With grateful acknowledgements to *Islington Family Service Unit* our
parent organization for all their help, support and guidance over
the years'

Contents

Preface

1 The start

2 In search of real live truants

3 The honeymoon

4 The kids — left to themselves

5 The staff — referees or reference points?

6 'This ain't a proper school'

7 The Centre of our lives

8 Back to school — who's fooling whom?

9 Growing up — all down to us

10 You can't please all of the people, all of the time

11 'There's no success like failure, and failure's no success at all'

12 A change of view

Bibliography

Preface

This book is a personal account of the first three years in the life of an education project set up by my wife and myself to cater for fifteen teenage truants.

Here and there in the narrative I express a number of strongly-held opinions about the state of our education system and the significance of the truancy problem. But I present very little statistical evidence to support my views. There is a reason for this omission.

Long before I left the Centre, I realised that I would need to write about it. I had also read enough of the available literature on the subject of truancy to know that if I were to present research evidence to support my views I would have to gather it myself. My rejection of existing literature was not based on any doubts about the academic credentials of the writers concerned nor even finally about the accuracy of the statistics given. It was more a question of basic assumptions about the nature of truancy that troubled me. I found myself unable to approach the subject as a study in psycho-social abnormality. Answers I believed were more likely to arise from the question 'Why have schools failed to meet the needs of these children?' than 'Why have these children failed to cope with the demands of school?'

As it transpired I was not to get the chance to conduct my own research. Everywhere I went for support I was told the same things: truancy is a very sensitive subject; the schools will not allow you in; your basic assumptions about the problem are very threatening to education authorities. I gave up and enrolled instead on an MSc course to study the existing literature further. My conclusions afterwards were little altered. There were books that encouraged and books that enraged me (at the end of this book there is a brief list of them) but I had, I felt, no choice but to write my own, without corroborating evidence. I fully believe that the evidence is there. If reading this book gives someone the encouragement necessary to begin searching for it, then something vitally useful will have been achieved.

My narrative requires, however, some kind of factual setting — even if the 'facts' have to be treated with caution. On 17 January,

1974, the Department of Education and Science conducted a spot check on the attendance of 3 886 000 pupils in England and Wales: 384 000 were found to be absent; 87 000 of that number were deemed absent 'for no good reason'.

Assuming that the sample chosen was fairly representative of tne whole school population we arrive at a national truancy figure of about 2.25 per cent. That is not, unfortunately, a very helpful way of judging the true extent of the truancy problem. Behind that overall percentage lie very substantial variations in the level of truancy in different schools, in different areas. Rough generalisations about the pattern of that variation would run as follows: truancy is higher in inner urban areas, higher in schools with catchment areas with large concentrations of pupils from social classes IV and V. A typical suburban grammar school might well claim a truancy rate of less than 0.5 per cent, while an inner urban comprehensive in an area of high social and economic stress might suffer truancy at the rate of 6 per cent or more. A spot check on attendance, conducted in 1971, in one Islington comprehensive revealed, for instance, 13 per cent truancy on the basis of the school register but found that a further 5 per cent of pupils had disappeared after getting their 'mark'.

Generalising on the basis of such spot-check figures is obviously dangerous and misleading. Schools in apparently similar areas may show very different levels of truancy. Truancy doesn't run at a constant level throughout the school year — or even through any given school week. Spot checks conducted on cold winter days will find many more children in school than checks done during fine summer months. The criteria used for determining what constitutes 'justifiable absence' may vary. An official survey of all attendance in one outer London borough demonstrates this very clearly. A school-by-school breakdown of the survey (conducted on one day in January 1974) shows that the proportion of all absence reckoned to be 'for no good reason' varied substantially. Some schools gave the proportion of absences deemed 'unreasonable' as high as 62 per cent, others returned figures as low as 5 per cent. Schools with similar levels of *overall* absence showed very different numbers of children as 'truant'. The only reasonable explanation for these differences is that some schools were much less strict about the excuses they accepted than others.

Within any given school the amount of truancy varies greatly between different 'years' and different academic streams. Truancy in the fourteen age group may be as much as 50 per cent higher than in the thirteen age group, and 70 per cent higher in the fifteen age group than in the fourteen. Overall, truancy will also tend to be higher the lower the academic level, perhaps as much as five or six times as high in the E and F streams as in the A or B streams in some schools.

The more detailed the analysis of the extent of the problem becomes, the more difficult it is to obtain accurate measurement. What proportion of truancy can be reckoned as chronic (children absent from school for say 60—70 per cent of the time) is very hard to assess. Some London schools of a thousand pupils might admit to having twenty to thirty chronic truants on their registers at any one time. There is a marked and understandable reluctance on the part of individual schools and education authorities to give precise figures. One thing, however, will be quite clear to anyone who has read the newspapers or watched TV over the last three or four years: the problem is serious, and few urban education authorities would be able to say they had the answer to it.

The Education Welfare Service whose responsibility it is, in most areas, to enforce school attendance has few resources at its disposal to meet the problem. Court action against parents or children is frequently ineffective. Providing casework for truants is rarely sufficient to bring about a return to school. Placing children in Care or finding boarding schools willing to take them is usually impractical or inappropriate. Education Authorities have thus been forced over the last five years or so to contemplate the possibilities of providing some form of alternative education for chronic truants. The Centre which forms the subject of this book is only one of the alternative education projects in London. Since the Centre opened in December 1971 some dozen other roughly similar projects have been started in other areas of the city. The future of such projects is precarious for reasons which I trust this book will make clear. But one fact is certain: even if there were to be fifty 'Centres' in London the truancy problem would still be there — unresolved.

One last prefatory word. The kids at the Centre wanted this book to be written. The possibility of unpleasant publicity did not disturb them. They wanted their first names to be used, unchanged, but felt that surnames where they appear should be altered for the sake of their families who had not chosen to be involved in the Centre. The Centre staff, past and present, also agreed that the book should be written. But I must stress that the views expressed about the Centre itself and the state of education generally are wholly my own. The Centre as it is now must be judged on its present merits.

How . . .

How are we born to be invisible? Well we aren't born to be invisible, we have to take some sort of tonic. Correction . . . we are born to be invisible if we have invisible parents. Now to get invisible, you must either go to your doctor or go to the chemist. But wait a 'mo', the chemist will not give you that tonic if you just want to get out of work, or get off school, he will only give you the tonic if for some reason you want to be invisible . . . if you are being followed by some evil crook he just might give you some.

It will stay for about four hours, but if you take the whole bottle you will automatically stay invisible, and if you stay invisible we will not be able to find you.

How and what do you do if you are invisible? Well you go to your psychiatrist, and he will give you a sort of bell to ring if you are in trouble, and he will come to your aid, and will give you some brandy, which will restore your normal self, and if it doesn't you are in trouble.

. . . . To make you invisible you will need some tonic, which will make you invisible, and to be invisible you will need invisible parents, who were born to be invisible.

Roy

1 The start

When you've answered the obvious question about 'How did you start?' (a euphemism for 'How the hell did you get into this crazy game?') fifty times, a distinct note of romanticism begins to appear in the story. It would be so much nicer to talk about long years of gathering anger, painstaking evolution of concepts, a wealth of corroborating personal experience. The creation of the Centre would then be seen as a just reward for time served in the wilderness, suffering blank bureaucratic refusals and broken promises of support. But it wasn't like that and I am not enough of a masochist to wish that it had been. In fact I will try to argue later that, in retrospect, I can see many advantages in our disgustingly easy early progress.

'My wife was working as a teacher in a secondary school. I was working as a family caseworker in Islington. From our different viewpoints we became increasingly concerned about the same problem — the children who gained little from the existing school system. So we decided to set up the Centre.' Very neat, factually accurate — but very misleading. Ange's school wasn't a depressed inner urban comprehensive, seething with violence and truancy. It was a very proper girls' grammar school in Ilford. Her direct experience of 'social problems' was confined to one poor scapegoated girl with a neurotic home and a small-scale drugs problem. Certainly, in many ways, that one experience gave cause enough for concern. Ange was politely told to stop meddling in matters beyond her professional scope. As the one teacher known to have any relationship with the girl, she was neither told nor consulted when the decision was made to exclude this bad influence from the school. But she knew nothing of truancy or classroom anarchy at first hand. I could claim to know something about truancy — or rather one end of the problem. Of the twenty-one school-age children on my caseload, there were eight or nine regular truants. With most of them I went through the humiliating experience of giving a punitive lift to school. I had to watch them squirming nervously around in the passenger seat, eyeing me cynically while I searched desperately for comforting platitudes to justify their attendance at school. It was humiliating because I had nothing to offer them, not even the dubious benefit of my experience. I had no experience. I knew nothing at all about what the kids I was supposed to care for had to face inside the school gates. On the few occasions I dared to venture into school myself I felt nervous, anonymous and ignorant. All I possessed was an instinct that there was little in their schools to interest or help the kids.

It didn't seem that I was much more help to them when I visited the family at home. I was there, apparently, chiefly to support Mum. The kids were usually thrown out or plugged into the TV to prevent irrelevant interruptions to Mum's tales of woe. Their only function was to serve as walking examples of bad clothing, bad health or bad behaviour — props to the argument. It isn't a question of the gross selfishness of mothers: they are fully entitled to demand a heavy share of undivided attention and sympathy. All I am saying is that, *I* could not, and cannot, accept that the strong mother-bias in division of labour was the most productive use of my energies. I could see that years spent largely helping the parents might ease their unhappiness to some degree, and might in the long term benefit the children too. But it seemed too slow, too indirect an approach to be effective as genuine prevention. While the parents are growing gradually towards some form of happiness, their children are speeding through stages of growth, absorbing influences, moulding their lives, fixing their limits. By the time the parents are happy enough to help their children, it may well be too late. The damage has been done, their lives hardened against positive change. For me it seemed logical, then, to work where the chance of effective help was highest — with the kids. Taking them on outings wasn't enough. Setting up after-school hours clubs wasn't enough. Family group sessions, however good, still left them without support they could call their own. And school, technically the most important potential source of care and support, seemed to fill most of the kids with a sense of profound boredom at best, terror at worst.

To set up our own school was the obvious answer. We had no real idea of what form it should take or of how we would 'help' the kids. We had no criteria of ideal alternative education by which to judge the existing school system — even supposing we had had a clear image of its failures. We could see no way of magically knowing the answers to all these questions except by doing the job, and finding out what we thought as we went along. If this version of how we started sounds implausibly short of motive, then that's probably because the account is incomplete. Few people would be mad enough to start their own project, with all its attendant agonies, just because 'it seemed like a logical thing to do'. Somewhere behind all the rationalisations there has to be a powerful force of self-interest.

No idea, centre, worker will survive for long, however good, without it.

In our case the motive was threefold. First, that we wanted to work together and had found when we had tried it before that our self-confidence was boosted by mutual support. Secondly, that we simply wanted to make something of our own, not to spend our working lives within someone else's ill-fitting definition of our capabilities. And thirdly we needed to feel really involved in other people's lives, close enough to be needed and visibly useful. Not, to be sure, a very decorative array of personal reasons but then there are very few challengers for the Purity of Soul prize.

The moral (if there is one) of our easy progress from initial idea to actual practice is probably a modification to the old 'Fools rush in' adage. Not only, it seems, do fools rush in, but they also stand a better chance than many of the highly experienced angels of getting away with it, because no one takes them seriously. As far as the Education Authority were concerned we certainly didn't need to be taken very seriously. We were carrying no political placards, were happily very short of damaging factual ammunition and were backed, not by the professionally-threatening might of a Social Services department, but by a very small voluntary agency. Just a 'nice' enthusiastic young couple, in fact. The other factor in our favour was pure luck. With all the wonderful scientific systems we have, the statistics, the social policy planning, what actually happens, who gets the money and who doesn't has as much to do with accident and coincidence as with anything else. We were in the right place at the right time. The Inner London Education Authority were beginning to be alarmed by their growing truancy figures. The Urban Aid decision-makers liked the idea of someone actually doing something called Intermediate Treatment rather than just talking about it. Perhaps for all I know, there was some more obscure piece of luck operating.

Writing our project proposal was undoubtedly the most painless part of the operation. It is so much easier to concoct the kind of neat theory required for funding applications from a position of relative ignorance. We were not inhibited by thoughts of how great the disparity would probably be between theory and practice. The awful moment when we would have to apply our theory seemed so distant. In moments of panic we comforted each other by remembering how unlikely it was that we would ever have to face that moment. Rereading that original document now is an embarrassing experience. All that naive use of fine-sounding terminology: 'therapeutic community', 'phased reintegration after an intensive period of personal, social and academic rebuilding'. In the event there was to be no 'phased reintegration', 'rebuilding' turned out to be a pathetically inadequate term for a very complex reality. The point, however, is not whether what we said was later proved 'true', but whether it worked, at the time, as a key to the answer.

We started thinking about the idea in December 1970. By March 1971 our application for Urban Aid was off on its long journey to the Home Office with Social Service Department blessing. We then turned our attention to the business of obtaining ILEA approval. Our first discussions at divisional office level were discouraging. Yes, it sounded like a good idea in principle . . . but should non-attenders be rewarded like this for their behaviour? Wouldn't other pupils who had never transgressed feel it to be unfair? Would the children ever go back to normal school after a period of such luxury treatment? 'And, quite frankly, Mr Grunsell, I can only think of half a dozen children in the whole borough who could possibly benefit from what you're offering'. I could have thought of more children than that on my own tiny caseload, but didn't say so. It was agreed that the proposal would be forwarded to County Hall for consideration. We weren't very hopeful. The agreement had been lukewarm, more a matter of procedure than support. We began to realise what being threatening meant. Our half-baked idea obviously represented a threat to the Education Welfare Service fighting as it was (and is) a largely losing battle against a steadily rising army of truants — numbering rather more than six. We were treading on already sensitive toes and were accordingly being warned off. Two months passed and no summons came from County Hall. Extra push was needed, and found, in the form of one of our Divisional Inspectors who, conveniently enough, carried an additional responsibility for special centres. He proved to be our chief backer within the ILEA. Without his protection I doubt if we would have either started or remained in business. Having found our back door, we were soon called to a meeting in County Hall.

After half an hour of unpleasant leading questions from Inspectors, Chief Educational Psychologists and the like, we felt like stopping the game. 'OK, we give up. It was just a joke, anyway. For a start we can't tell you whether our treatment would be intended primarily for school-phobias because we've never seen one.' There could be no such let-out. We blundered on trying at all costs to avoid being pinned down to precise definitions of what we would be doing and to whom. It was the best thing we could have done. At the time our main motive was the need to disguise our enormous ignorance in vagueness. In retrospect we have become highly conscious of how many so-called experiments have been doomed from the outset by over-tight definitions. An experiment cannot fulfil its purpose unless it is allowed flexibility. And flexibility is not the strong point of large-scale bureaucracies.

Yet, amazingly, after two hours of interrogation, the answer was 'yes' — and moreover 'yes' as a full-time alternative to school. At the time the conditions of approval seemed to us to be surprisingly lenient. The chief requirement was that we should aim at returning our pupils to normal school within a year. We were only to take children referred by our two designated schools. The Education Authority would employ two teachers to be allocated to the project from permanent Divisional staff. We felt happy enough to accept a referral system. That the teachers should be paid by the Education Authority we recognised as an important principle. The risk that the piper might insist on calling the tune was one we had to accept. The requirement that children be returned to school we welcomed at the time as a positive challenge. Only later were we to see it in a very different light.

From then on it was mostly downhill. Urban Aid gave us the full £8000 per year for five years that we had asked for — a figure that had been arrived at by adding 33 per cent to the figure we reckoned we needed. In September we approached the Housing department for a short-life property. After some misgivings — 'You wouldn't want us to give you a house intended for homeless families, would you?' — they agreed in principle but left the search for suitable premises to us. Driving endlessly round the half-derelict streets of North Islington, we realised what a blitzed and desperate area we had chosen. Eventually, 6 Cromartie Road came on to our list of likely houses. 'Two years' life. To be demolished for a link road.' (Five years later it is still there, awaiting rehabilitation — we were lucky again.) It was enough. We took it for the nominal rent of £1 per month.

While the house was being repaired (largely a matter of making good the damage done during eighteen months of standing empty) we went through the most superficial round of local introductions. The Heads of the two schools we were to serve had us to lunch. We had been imposed on them from on high. There was no reason why they should have been particularly enthusiastic. Being chosen as suitable schools for our project meant a public recognition of their truancy problem. Hardly a compliment. Beneath the surface welcome, their reactions seemed to be a mixture of suspicion, caution and pity (we were patently suckers). In a fit of bonhommie one of our Heads invited us to spend the day at their rural studies centre in Essex. We were much impressed — though not quite in the way intended — by the opulence of the place: parquet floors, Sanderson curtains et al., a good £50 000 worth. We were instantly cured of our awe over our mere £8000 and our guilt at spending £800 of it on repairs and decoration. We were struck by the restrictive atmosphere in which all activity was designed to be strictly 'educational'. Remarks were made such as 'It's so difficult to stop them phoning home for the football results', and 'The children really respect the standards here', 'We've only had one piece of graffitti since we opened'. To us the kids seemed intimidated rather than respectful. If they enjoyed it, it was largely in spite of the regime rather than because of it. It was encouraging to find that, however little we knew positively what we wanted, at least we possessed a strong instinct that it wasn't that kind of narrow 'educational experience'. 'Look at these lock-gates', a group were told, 'Try to memorise how they work. You'll have to write an essay on it later which will be useful for O-level.'

Other attempts on our part to get ideas and advice were less encouraging. At the Tavistock Clinic we were told that all truancy was an 'encapsulation of some form of personal disorder' — a phrase which left us with a curious image of truants as a species of walking virus. There was much sage wagging of heads when we admitted that we hadn't envisaged having a consultant psychologist on permanent call. From the radical education fringe the message was that we had already sold out by agreeing to return the kids to school, by not insisting on the right of self-referral. Those who saw the project in terms of treatment informed us that we had no hope of successfully reintegrating our truants without a detailed programme of intensive therapy. The nearer we got to the dreaded Day One, the more confused we became. In self-defence we listened less and less to the advice we were given. I can now recall only one accurate remark from a would-be adviser at the time: 'You're obviously not the slightest bit interested in any advice. It's your brain-child. You just want to get started.'

We needed a second teacher. Getting the right person for an existing, well-defined job is difficult enough. What we were trying to do was find someone who was in tune with ideas we only half-possessed and could only half express, for a job we couldn't define. A number of people presented themselves with ideas and hang-ups of their own to fill the vacuum in our thinking. The hesitancy and caution with which we treated all approaches were sufficient to drive most of them away. Pete Davis kept on coming. His attitudes were, unlike ours, based on direct school experience. In his previous teaching post he had been forbidden to take his class to see *Hair* during school hours and warned off taking them in his own time ('Remember that I have to write your reference'). Characteristically, he had retaliated by mounting his own production of *Hair* with his class. His Head was unamused and Pete had left the job in search of a teaching context where more of his energy could be used in teaching rather than in a war of attrition against restrictive structures. He wasn't, however, on an embittered rebound. He shared our lack of dogma, not to say confusion. As the Centre grew and our dogmatism with it, Pete's constant pragmatism came to be seen as a much-needed counterbalance.

By now I must have succeeded in creating a barely credible image of our beginnings — a saga of happy muddle and confusion. The criticism is obvious: if we had been as uncertain as I have claimed we would never have got started. I am emphatically not trying to sing the praises of the Great British Amateur Tradition. I might have avoided giving that impression by talking more of pragmatism than of uncertainty. With hindsight I could, it is true, interpret many of our decisions and indecisions as motivated by a proper open-minded caution. It is now possible to see that many of the ideas we came to practise and articulate were already in our minds waiting to be tested. But I prefer to let my stress stand as a useful underlining to the point I want to make. The fact that we were left largely alone and undirected to sort out and test our ideas was not, I believe, merely a lucky bonus. It was crucial to whatever measure of success we achieved. It meant that we were not rushed into making irreversible decisions about the structure of the project based purely on theory, but rather that, knowing how tentative our initial structure had been, we were more willing to make changes. Most important of all, it meant that whatever we had was ours. It being our creation (good, bad and ugly) we were prepared to fight that much harder for its survival. If new projects show a high casualty rate, the failure may well be not in the planning or the concept, but in the lack of opportunity for the development of the level of personal commitment in the staff necessary for their survival.

2 In search of real live truants

We had a house, we had the money. All we needed was a few real truants to put us in business. But we weren't exactly overwhelmed by advance bookings and could hardly claim to be in the best position to start touting for trade. We were looking for unknown customers for an unknown service. The schools were to be the referring agents, we had said; we wanted them to feel involved with the truants we took from them. But when we sat down for lunch with the year masters in one of our schools we began to appreciate the true awkwardness of our position for the first time.

The Headmaster explained to the assembled company that these two young people had decided to offer help with the school's truants, and that he was sure the staff would welcome this additional service. After the obligatory round of encouraging smiles, the conversation settled on a search for names of possible candidates. Within five minutes we were hearing graphic descriptions of the school's most spectacular trouble-makers: that big West Indian girl who had wrecked 4B; the dreaded child from 3F who was currently boss of the playground protection racket. Everyone knew them, and had their own gruesome anecdotes to add to the story. These were the kids they urgently needed help with. But, no, they wouldn't be appropriate referrals, would they, because, unfortunately, they had a nasty habit of coming to school regularly. Trying to think of the kids who didn't was a much more laborious business. Names were provided. Other staff didn't know, couldn't remember what the kids looked like. An effort of memory seemed, in most cases, to produce some reason for deeming the referral inappropriate: in this case, it was only because Mum was seriously ill, in that case there was a concerned teacher trying to get the kid to Child Guidance.

We wondered if our vision of bands of truants roaming the streets had been pure imagination on our part. We knew, however, that it wasn't. Two kinds of explanation presented themselves to us. It was obvious, for one, that no one knew much about the truants. By definition, there was every reason for that. The time that these teachers had available for pastoral case duties was patently insufficient even for the sheep who stayed in the fold, let alone those that were lost. Inevitably it was the noisiest members of the flock who received most attention. There was a strong temptation for these endlessly harrassed people to feel an unprofessional gratitude for any reduction in the size of their flock. The other source of explanation followed naturally. Our quest for customers acted as an unwelcome reminder of problems the teachers would much rather forget. We were treading on already highly sensitive toes. These were, in the majority, experienced and dedicated staff well aware of the inadequacies of their school who had to fight for security. No one can be expected to set about happily kicking away the assumptions of twenty years hard labour — particularly not at the behest of a couple of fresh-faced amateurs. None of these things could be, or were, said. Two or three names remained as possibles at the end of the lunch. We left with best wishes all round and very little more of an idea of what our truants looked like.

Of course, we'd done our homework: selected readings from the surprisingly slim body of literature on the subject of truancy. But we were not much the wiser. Most of what we read focused on family pathology seen from the standpoint of individual casework, casework following the methods and principles of Child Guidance Clinics. Walking symptoms of neurotic disorder are difficult to visualise. How could we create an environment for truants unless we knew how they, as people, felt about school, about their families?

From available evidence, it seemed that there were almost as many types of truant as there are types of personality. However, what did emerge was that truants seemed to be considered in two fairly distinct categories. Either they were 'sick' (from families with somewhat middle-class aspirations, perhaps) and therefore deserving of specialised help. Or they were 'bad', that is they were from socially maladjusted backgrounds and needed (deserved, though in a rather different sense from the first category) appropriate provision through the courts or from social workers. Ideologically, that was an image we were reluctant to accept. But equally, what little we knew and had read didn't fit with the alternative vision of truants as the vanguard of educational revolution either.

What we wanted was some real kids with whom we could work out our confusion. Already forewarned by our experience in visiting the schools, we were grateful for what we got: seven referrals, all from Archway school where we had felt there was a much greater underlying hostility to our project. Not surprisingly, therefore, we were highly suspicious, wondering what state of end-of-the-line desperation had driven the school to offer these seven kids. As it transpired we were quite right — those seven, and many more that followed, *were* kids at the end of the line for whom no one could find any provision with any chance of success. We could hardly complain, having decided to start the project precisely because we believed there was a huge gap in provision for truants, if we found ourselves used in this way. As it was, most of the first seven fitted with the very sketchy criteria we had laid down for referral: they had two years of school left to run which gave us time, in theory, to effect their reintegration; their homes seemed, on paper at least, sufficiently stable to allow us to establish a working relationship with the family; we even had a balance of sexes in the referrals to enable us to establish our mixed group. And, most important of all, they were all, without question, actual truants.

We had imagined that we would be able to build our group by careful and well-informed selection. We wanted a subtle balance of personalities and talents and believed that, by the time any kid got as far as referral to us, there would inevitably be a wealth of relevant observation on which to base our judgements. The schools had already proved that, frequently, they had scant knowledge about their truants, but we were not deterred: somebody else must have the information we wanted. Looking quickly at the papers we received it appeared at first as though this was true. There wasn't much that could help us on the school referral form itself — but, then, we had soon recognised that we had made a bad job of designing the form, had asked the wrong questions and left no room for teachers to answer the right ones for themselves. We had reports from other agencies, however, to make up the gaps: Education Welfare, Social Services, Child Guidance reports. We began reading in search of 'the Reason' for each kid's truancy and finished reading with the strong feeling that somehow it was missing. Comments always seemed to give descriptive details from the edge of the problem, not reasons from the middle: 'a nice enough lad', 'seems depressed and apathetic when his attendance is mentioned', 'apart from school attendance, he seems obedient enough', 'he could think of nothing, when asked, that interested him at school', 'unable to give reasons for his truancy, says it's just a bad habit he's got into', 'parents claim to be anxious, but appear to have given up caring. I suspect collusion.' What 'appeared' and 'seemed' to be true *appeared* to be mostly negative.

The authors of those comments were not myopic fools. We had little to add to what they said after our first round of visits to the homes of the kids referred to us. Our first meeting with Mike, not one of those original seven, would serve as an example. The family assembled for battle, with Mum in the middle commanding the lines of defence. For the fourteenth or fortieth time her boys were in trouble for truancy which meant that she was under attack for being a bad mother. The obvious strategy was to present a tight front, offering as little for attack as possible and minimising the length of the battle by giving the impression of early surrender. Put less melodramatically, she had her boys well drilled in the art of giving the 'right' answers. We settled down in the ruins of a front room while the boys hurriedly swept coal off the carpet, and did our friendly piece about what the Centre had to offer. When we asked Mike the inevitable 'Why?' what we got was, 'Dunno'. Mum had gathered enough from what we had said to realise that we might be a chance to avoid court again, in which case 'Dunno' was the wrong answer because it implied that Mike was uncooperative. With a quick verbal prompt, Mike switched tracks. 'Well, I bunked off the once and I was scared to go back the next day and it just sort of got worse from then. It's just a bad habit I've got into, I suppose.' And a little more prodding from Mum produced some suitable phrase about 'needing a fresh start'. Mum clinched the manoeuvre with 'Ah, he'd leap at the chance of a place like yours, wouldn't you, Mike?' The only leaping Mike seemed eager to perform was out of the window and off down the road.

Naturally we could see more in the situation than just that. Throughout the interview Dad sat by the fire, sucked his pipe and said nothing at all. Clearly it was a mother-dominated family, we decided, and Mike was a very frightened kid. There was enough information there for intelligent guesswork about reasons for truancy. But it was far from clear why he ran out of apparently friendly classes, claiming he felt 'got at', and away from the sympathetic year master who let him sit in his office. If our contact had ended with that visit, we would never have discovered that he provoked persecution by other kids, that he was terrified of men, that he loved reading, was endlessly fascinated by science, that he was capable of immense toughness and courage.

Much the same could be said of our other kids. The school report noted that A.J., who was among our first referrals 'is exceedingly withdrawn and detached and unnaturally quiet for a boy of his age'. Later chapters will show A.J. as the most aggressive and sociable kid who ever reached the Centre. An educational psychologist's report on Tony commented: 'It was difficult to find anything that really did interest Tony'. At the Centre he proved to be very easy to interest, perceptive, knowledgeable and extremely hard-working. Elsewhere in that same report he was described as 'a disruptive influence . . . given to violent outbursts . . . beating up other children and displaying aggression generally' — a far more apt description of

A.J. Yet at the time it had Pete and I wondering whether we should enrol for karate classes. In his two years with us Tony never once beat up anyone — staff or pupil.

I'm not claiming miracle cures or pouring ridicule on the authors of these reports, merely pointing to a simple fact: that the majority of teachers and social workers have little chance of seeing these kids as whole people. The context in which they meet produces, for the most part, only the negative and defensive elements in their character. The opportunity to know or demonstrate positive choice is limited by the concentration on their rejection of school. They are, after all, truants, whose arts of self-defence induce deception, withdrawal and avoidance. Little wonder, then, that we found ourselves dealing with an unknown race.

Coming to the centre . . .

When I was told that I was going to the Centre I didn't like the idea. I didn't really want to come to the Centre. I thought about changing schools and classes which I have always had to do for different reasons. But I knew it was a good school and different people say that you don't learn in that school. But it's wrong. Because when I first went there I liked the school straightaway and you do learn here, you get a lot of help here when you need it. I didn't really feel scared or anything when I first come because I knew all the kids here and the teachers and I knew all the kids that had come to this school and had left.

Doreen

Your actual truant

To state the obvious: there is no such animal as the average truant. The five we chose from the first seven referrals were all very different individuals. Of course, we could apply a few shorthand labels: Fran and Paul — paranoid, over-protective parents, consequently fear-ridden about the outside world; Jimmy — victim of marital manipulation, over-indulged by lonely mother; A.J. — indulgent mother, unable to relate to father, insecure sense of his own identity; Sylve — neurotic family, extremely deprived of love. And so on. It's an almost immoral exercise. They must speak for themselves in later chapters. But perhaps it is worth giving just one portrait — not of the worst truant, the most deprived, the most delinquent, but of a kid called Jamie who, if he was any one thing, was, more than most, a victim.

Jamie lived some two hundred metres from the Centre along the hill in a block of redbrick flats created by an architect whose previous experience must have been the design of penal institutions. Their main features were long, windy galleries punctuated by Council regulation purple doors facing into a bare concrete yard ruled by a tyrannical caretaker. Jamie's flat was on the top, looking out over London — a loveless, hopeless home. 'It wasn't that good, even when we first met. It just happened one night when we had a bit to drink. There she was, expecting. So we got married. It seemed the only thing to do. And then the other two came along. It seems fucking stupid saying it like that, but that's how it was — for the sake of the kids is what we said. 'Course there's nothing here now. Never was, I suppose.' Jamie's dad knew well enough, and tried his best to care: a morning cup of tea for Jamie when he wasn't on early shift, new clothes when he was lucky on the horses, a drink from the pub in the evening and promises of holidays he never managed to keep. His mum made him promises too when things were going well with the boyfriend — summer at Butlins or a house in the country. But most of the time Jamie was just a bloody nuisance.

So Jamie grew up alone in his own world. A weedy kid, he was a natural victim for every school Mafia. Threatened and blackmailed, unable to trust the teachers for protection, he quietly withdrew. When the complaining letters came from school he reached them first and threw them away. When the School Board man came in the morning, he stayed safely asleep. When he came in the evening, his parents were out. When they finally found out, they cared but could do nothing. Dad was on earlies, Mum was living with the boyfriend, the elder daughters never got up till midday. Nothing changed. Jamie wasn't an urgent case, not a serious delinquent. He was fed and clothed after a fashion, neglected in a slow deadly way that wouldn't bring his case to court. So he wandered.

Down the hill from the Centre the GLC were destroying a square mile of London for redevelopment. It looked like a bad case of saturation bombing. For Jamie, it was the stage-set for one of his dreams. Exploring the ruined houses looking for the old and the valuable, there was always a magic chance he would find the diamond that would buy him and his dad out of their miserable flat. For the demolition boys engaged in licenced looting, he was a pain in the neck, a dopey kid hanging around, getting in their way. In the eyes of the few old residents left in the area, he was just adding insult to injury — not only had their nice neighbourhood been smashed to pieces, but they had to suffer the delinquent scum of London dumped on their doorstep as well. Up above the Centre, the folks who live on the hill were just as hostile. The tenants of the new estate were on the make. Jamie, shambling up through their clean new corridors, was an invasion from a world they were trying to escape — a walking example of urban squalor. Across the road at the top of the hill, it was quiet civilised Highgate where Jamie would be picked up in five minutes flat by any patrolling Panda car. Behind his estate on the old railway line, he was safest. As long as he avoided the little bands of mickey-taking glue-sniffers and the expeditions setting off for a quick raid on 'Woolies', he could be at peace.

He wasn't a misunderstood saint. He did the gas meter regularly to buy friends among the little kids in the yard. His paper dart experiments littered the flats and enraged the caretaker. He pinched wood from the bowling green fence, lit fires on waste ground and gave the Fire Brigade a fair bit of practice. Much of what he did seemed meaningless and infuriating to his neighbours and his parents. The woman in the flat below didn't realise that the string dangling past her balcony was Jamie's method of measuring the height of his flats. His collections of stones, old coins and assorted rubbish messed up the living room and got thrown away by his mum who never understood what private treasure they were to him. Long before he came to us he had lost the will and ability to tell anyone what he felt inside his head. He was a dead-end, dumb loser — your actual truant.

Jamie

Pete: *Do you think we have any rules here?*
Jamie: *Yes. No smoking in lessons . . . . and . . . . er no staying in after school.*
Pete: *Yes you can stay after school.*
Jamie: *No you can't. She chucks you out.*

3 The honeymoon

As with most honeymoon couples, it was acute mutual nervousness that kept us together during our first months. Neither side, kids or staff, knew whether the other really cared and if so how much. Neither side really wanted to know where the limits were going to be, since the discovery would inevitably mean conflict. Yet none of us could survive for long with the tension of not knowing. We stalked around one another, probing, withdrawing, compromising, edging towards the crunch.

For the kids it was obviously too good to be true. Only five of them with three adults all to themselves, a whole house of their own, and freedom. There had to be a catch. It wasn't freedom, as much as a very alarming vacuum. Predictably they tried to fill that space with their own expectations based on what they already knew. Something akin to the perfect primary school class. For the first three weeks up to the end of Christmas term they didn't try to smoke or swear, it was all 'Sir' and 'Miss'. They came willingly into lessons, accepted instructions without question, stayed quiet and unsupervised in the living room in breaks and lunch-hours while the teachers quite properly retired to the office. At three-forty-five, like other good schoolchildren, they trotted off home carrying their homework, homework they had asked to be given as a publicly recognisable symbol of the fact that they were at a proper school. It was just what they had always wanted: school without tears. Real lessons, real schoolwork, real teachers whom they could actually get to know. But no crowds or noise, no anxiety about where they were supposed to be, no gangs to intimidate them. The snag was that it meant pretending they were only seven years old.

We couldn't believe it either. These were five very difficult kids — the files said so. Of course we were three wonderful people, but it couldn't really be that easy. We had decided that two long morning lessons would be better than three or four short periods, to give the kids time to settle into subjects in a relaxed way. It seemed to work. They appeared to enjoy the less structured afternoons, the art, drama, hobbies, visits out. We hadn't honestly thought about homework till the kids suggested it. Preparing lunch each day with one of them certainly made it the warm friendly focal point for the group that we had intended. Cosy, in fact, more than warm. Given the need on both sides for security that cosiness was hardly surprising. We needed proof that we were able to give the intensive support we had talked so much about, just as the kids wanted reassurance in this fragile new relationship. Sensing and sharing our anxiety about its future, they worked hard to give it a strong identity. Nicknames rapidly evolved: we were all, it was decided, 'mongs' (short for mongrel, the local corruption of the word mongol). When a stray cat was found zipped into an airline bag on the railway line, it was named Mong and became the Centre cat. Four years and eighteen kittens later Mong is still there as a reminder of how much the first five helped in creating the Centre.

We were profoundly uneasy. The closeness was unhealthy and unreal. We recognised that limits would have to be placed on the relationships. But until we knew how much we could tolerate and the kids introduced into the Centre their true hellishly-muddled teenage lives, there was no way of finding those limits. Taking on more referrals would break the deadlock but our schools, rightly suspicious perhaps, were slow to offer new names. We had to wait.

The strained euphoria began to evaporate at the beginning of the spring term when we took the kids to Wales for four days, implementing our theory that termly trips away would bind the group together and widen their horizons of experience (a conventional enough philosophy). Given that the experience was of a cold, austere Youth Hostel in a bitter wet January, we got less than we asked for. We did get our first dose of reality, however. Smokers ourselves, it seemed hypocrisy to forbid them to smoke. The kids noticed, at last, that we didn't react to swearing. 'Sir' and 'Miss' disappeared — small symptoms of the changing awareness of how much of their outside lives the Centre could include. It began to include their apathy. We had our first experience of the world-famous 'I'm-not-getting-out-of-the-van-for-some-boring-old-castle' routine.

Back in the Centre there were other significant signs of change. Sally, our art teacher, had all her previous experience in primary schools, so that was how she ran her classes. At first the kids responded to this approach, encouraged it even, as a comforting bit of nostalgia. Gradually they began to resist: it was childish, boring. Why couldn't they make something useful like a go-kart? Alwyn's weekly drama class posed a more important threat. His aggressive acting-out technique was too much to take. The kids felt nowhere near safe enough to risk exposing so much about themselves. Wednesday mornings became routinely difficult. The knowledge that for two hours of the afternoon they were going to be actively encouraged to unleash all the furies they were trying so hard to contain for the rest of the week, meant a steady build-up of excitement and anxiety through the morning. Alwyn acquired scapegoat status.

There was plenty of warning of the trouble we could expect when the next three arrived. Our firstborn five were an ill-fitting bunch. Natural personal clashes were becoming noticeable. They needed a wider group to explore. But facing the prospect of displacement by 'second children' they were totally united in opposition. It would spoil the whole thing. They wouldn't get taught so well. It would be too crowded. The first time we had visitors in the Centre after school, they had barricaded themselves in the classroom, refusing to leave until the visitors had gone, so we were expecting something of what we got.

What we did get was a wholesale rebellion on the new kids' first day. It started with rumbles throughout the first lesson: 'What are the new kids doing downstairs? I bet you're not making them work'. 'They'll have it soft', 'They'll ruin it all, start fights. Then you'll get strict and it'll be just like ordinary school.' At break they edged round the new kids as though they were Frankenstein, Mohammed Ali and King Kong. And at the start of the second lesson they actually said 'No': they wouldn't do it, we couldn't make them, why should they do lessons at all, if they didn't come we'd have no Centre, no job. The honeymoon was over. We told them that if they wouldn't accept the terms offered, they should leave the building. They took the challenge and walked out. Theoretically we believed that our attitude had been the right one, that they had to act out the consequences of what they said. Actually we felt totally beaten and despairing. Our first group discussed tactics on the doorstep and then began pelting the house with mud from the building-site. We sat in the living room, trying to fake calm self-assurance, telling ourselves that total non-reaction was the most powerful weapon we had in this situation. Depriving the kids of a battle, we said, would force them to confront the real sources of their anger. Privately, Pete and I were fighting the strong desire to storm out into the street and thump the lot of them.

Out in the street the game was getting boring. When the workmen on the building-site began giving their own views on discipline, it gave the kids a convenient excuse to change targets. It was an unwise choice. Totally outclassed in the mud-slinging league, they retreated to the Centre for shelter. It was perhaps too easy a victory for us. Once inside again their insecurity found its voice. The routine had been broken. They wanted lunch. There was none — they hadn't made it. They had told the new kids that it was their Centre. At that moment it looked a shambles. Within ten minutes they were clearing up and preparing lunch.

What do you learn . . . ?

What do you like to learn in school?
Science . . . and how to make money.
Anything else?
Reading and writing.
Do you think they are important to learn?
Yes, of course I do. Not just for me, for everyone. Say when you leave school and go to work, they give you your money, your slip, you know. You can't read it out, you don't know how much you've got or anything, do you? And if you get some papers — say you get married, right? and you can't read and your wife says — read that for us — you'll be standing there and won't be able to read it.

Mark and Jamie

In trying, thus far, to give a narrative account of the Centre as though it were a unified entity, I have probably told many lies. There is no one perspective on events but a whole interrelated series. Working within a simple chronological framework implies a chain of causation that may well be phoney. The story as I have told it shows the first group rebellion as the neat climax of the inevitable process of mutual disillusionment. But it could equally serve as an example of the fight for group leadership that began soon after we opened and continued long after this supposedly crucial rebellion was forgotten. Or as an instance of the staff's naiveté in handling group feelings — I could even argue, with a fair degree of seriousness, that the outcome proved nothing about the efficiency of our laissez-faire tactics, but merely that the average workman can throw mud more accurately than the average kid. The last thing I want to do, however, is to embark on a treatise concerning the Unknowability of Final Truth. Working in the Centre we were frequently forced to make arbitrary decisions which cut across our awareness of all the different possible perspectives. Similarly in writing I must at this point abandon, for the sake of clarity, any attempt at integrated narrative. The compartments I create for different areas of the Centre experience are bound to be arbitrary and will, quite rightly, overlap. Analysis of the kids' relationships with each other is incomplete without a parallel view of how they related to the staff. The workings of the staff group had obvious repercussions on morale amongst the kids, which in turn affected the nature of teaching in the Centre — and so on round the chain. Indeed, one of the most basic principles of the Centre's existence was, and still is, that areas of interaction should *not* be fixed in any rigid structure: that teaching was not separable from social work, home visiting wasn't the sole responsibility of one specialist worker, the kids' views were as important as those of the staff. All of which makes my job of description that much harder. There is a brief chronology of events in the growth of the Centre on page 119.

At various points in what follows I focus on particular kids or events in a way that inevitably breaks across the chapter headings I have chosen to use. My excuse for doing this is simply that it is the only way I can find to reinforce the fact that those headings *are* only a matter of convenience.

4 The kids — left to themselves

It had been difficult enough with only five. Even with all the enforced group feeling of the early days we couldn't treat them just as a group. All five demanded to be treated as individuals on their own terms: Fran couldn't cope with group pressure, Sylve had to love or hate us to death, A.J. and Jimmy both had to be king, Paul demanded special protection from the staff against bullying and teasing. Where the hell did we start — or stop? But we had said fifteen not five as our maximum. We had to keep on building and to ignore our terrified imaginations. As the demands on our attention multiplied we had no choice but to learn the healthy virtue of minding our own business.

The first child jealousy crisis faded. Two months later, when two more kids arrived, the response was curiosity rather than hysteria: the advantages of having a larger group to explore and relate to had become clear. The first group's united front was rapidly submerged by a much more fluid, subtle series of cliques, alliances and oppositions, each kid pursuing his own form of 'social security'. The results were every bit as complicated and serious as the backstage affairs of the United Nations.

As the only two girls, Sylve and Fran had, gauche as they were, posed little threat to the boys. Teased mercilessly, they retreated to Ange's motherly protection for reassurance about their femininity. When Christine and Jane arrived, both very obviously real live women, the balance shifted. The result was two months of sex war. What had been designated the kids' room became, during three days of argument and negotiation, the boys' room. The girls set to work in the still-derelict basement to create a bigger and better girls' room. Fines for trespass were imposed, protocol for visiting agreed upon. Lessons became a battleground. Demands were made for separate girls' and boys' activities on Hobbies afternoons — boxing and football, sewing and cookery. But it wasn't that simple.

Simultaneously within and across the battle lines other kinds of manoeuvring were under way. Among the boys there was Paul seeking a status less dangerous than being ping-pong ball in A.J. and Jimmy's leadership match. With the arrival of Mike and Jamie he found a group to share his terror of and fascination for violence. This new clique developed their own style. In an average break-time they were usually to be found as a group apart, experimenting with candles and string, paper planes or chemicals, playing tag on the stairs. The girl—boy war was not their scene: it was other boys they feared, girls they hardly noticed at all.

The girls were just as divided. Sylve and Fran felt ambivalent about their allies. Inevitable comparison made Sylve aware of her crumpled assortment of clothes, Fran of her boy's voice and non-existent figure. Lady Jane with all her smart feminine poise was as much of a threat to them as the insults from the boys' camp. More and more of their time was spent trying to build up a reassuring relationship with Christine. And across the lines there were the fiercely protective family ties between Paul and Fran. Warfare could never go far before conflicting loyalties forced them to disengage.

The war lost its point. The kids could now see where their basic loyalties lay and turned their attention away from relating as a whole group to the business of consolidating their own cliques. A year later the unused girls' room became the Youth Club. Eighteen months later the boys' room was redecorated to become Ange's quiet room where our baby Leila slept during school hours.

The boy—girl war had been easy enough to justify in our own minds: good textbook stuff, a necessary stage in adolescent development. As whole group interaction disintegrated into a multitude of seemingly unrelated fragments, our assurance went with it. In the moments of exhausted after-school post-mortem, we struggled to find labels to give some semblance of sanity to the confusion. We couldn't honestly convince ourselves of their accuracy, but at the time we couldn't afford to admit it. So much that happened in an average day or week seemed like pure destruction, a sterile cycle of temporary alliances based on mutual hang-ups, followed by bitter argument, depression, regression and the making of new, equally temporary friendships. Psychological jungle warfare at its worst.

Paul's little group seemed to be fixed in infantile fantasy, hopelessly vulnerable to any outside influence. They were happy enough doing aerodynamic experiments with paper darts out of the office window, but when asked to clear up the resulting litter, they immediately retreated into obstinate sulks, five-year-old tantrums or hysterical paranoia about the awful violence Pete or I were about to unleash upon them. Every incident seemed to end the same way: Paul backing into a corner, hands over his ears, shouting 'Don't touch me. Don't come near me. If you lay a finger on me I'll get my dad, my auntie' (a dire threat) or the entire boot-boys brigade of North London armed with thermo-nuclear rockets. If it wasn't us, it was a whisper in the ear from A.J. that set them going. The harmless games would escalate: dangling string over the banisters became dropping nails over the banisters, experiments with chemicals became the manufacture of stink-bombs. When the red light went on for approaching limits, the backstage manipulators disappeared from the scene of the crime, leaving our three heroes to take the fall. Results as before. They didn't seem to be testing our different limits. It was the same tedious brick wall every time.

It would have seemed less depressing if they had, at least, maintained loyalty to each other but they were champion back-stabbers as well. Every week contained one or more touching little example of rock-bottom betrayal. Paul and Mike would agree to isolate their dear friend Jamie so they could get the maximum humour out of showing him to be pathetic and vulnerable. Or Mike and Jamie would lie their way out of criminal involvement, and sit piously in the audience watching Paul take the rap. But top prize for betrayal undoubtedly went to Sylve and Fran. They had recognised each other very accurately from the start. They saw in each other the same terror of growing up into women, the longing to stay secure as little girls protected by the all-loving mums neither of them had, the desperate need to have close girl friends to support them. Yet the sheer desperation of their own individual needs overruled all that mutual sympathy. In the battle for friends it was no holds barred. As soon as Sylve began visiting Christine in her flat after school, Fran moved in to sabotage her fragile friendship: passing secrets in a quiet corner after lunch — 'Did Christine know what Sylve had said about her being a slut?' Sylve was used to losing friends and well versed in the art of retaliation. Primed with a few fantasies about how Fran was leading poor Sylve astray, her mum would ban further contact between the girls. It only needed a similar decree from Fran's mum for the mutual destruction to be complete. With both of them deeply hurt and lonely, negotiations for friendship would begin once again. Once the bond was re-established, the whole sad cycle could start another turn. As fast as they built up trust, they demolished it. Looking back over the months, we could see little sign of anything resembling a good relationship.

Even those not directly featured in this parade of humanity at its spectacular worst were affected by it. Christine was no less desperate for friendship than Sylve and Fran. But she was trapped inside the intense depression of being old at fifteen, the classic anxious worn-out mum to a drunken father and a family of young brothers and sisters. Because she felt too paralysed to seek out friends she was forced to sit and wait for courtship. And what she got was Sylve and Fran, clinging to her, using her, rejecting her — giving her nothing.

Christine was a loser in the game without even joining it. Meanwhile Jane and Tony may not have lost much, but they gained little either. Jane was strong enough to take the ridicule — 'Lady Jane, all airs and graces, stuck-up little bitch'. Its effect, however, was to drive her further into detachment from the other kids, into deeper dreams about being a lady of style and refinement, living in a little white cottage in rural bliss. And Tony just watched, with a look of pitying amusement, keeping out of his very private world as much of the noise and chaos as he could.

If what I've just described wasn't something of a one-sided caricature of what actually happened during our first six months, we would all have resigned and sought retraining as chartered accountants. But it is accurate enough to explain why we were frequently in a state of near-despair. So much of what we lived through seemed to prove the case of the believers in 'strong discipline and guidance' — education as a means of civilising the barbaric young. Our role looked suspiciously like that of a Red Cross unit on the edge of a battlefield. We were there only to patch up the wounded and push them back into a conflict in which there was no possibility of productive outcome. By active intervention we might be able to curb some of the painful excesses, but the warfare would still be just as sterile as before. So much for our trite theory about 'creating an environment where the children could explore and develop their capacity for productive social involvement'. But we couldn't give up quite that easily. With every additional dose of hell, we became more bloody-minded in our determination to make it work.

It did begin to work and it has gone on working. There were no miracle transformations involved. If there had been, it would be a simple enough exercise to prove what we know to be true, namely that, given the space and the help, the kids can become happier. As it is, the process of change is much too subtle and complex to be glaringly self-evident to an uninvolved observer. A visitor for the day, watching with horror the progress of a blazing row between Fran and Sylve wouldn't draw much consolation from being told, 'Ah, but you should have seen them three months ago! If you watch carefully, you'll see that *now* they can actually talk about the row afterwards'. We are left, therefore, wide open to the accusation that we merely saw what we wished to see, that human behaviour can be interpreted any way you like. I deny it.

The feuds went on. Our mistake had been in imagining that the kids were as vulnerable to direct personal attack as we were. The feelings being expressed in a row during which Sylve and Fran told each other that they were lying, cheating, smelly, ugly little tarts may have been no stronger than what we felt in our own relationships.

But being used to our own more devious means of attack, the witty back-handers, destructive character analyses, etc., we felt their style to be much more damaging. The kids gradually began to show us that they were much tougher than we had ever realised. At the end of each bitter round they were still sufficiently intact to learn something from the hell they inflicted on each other.

The Paul-Mike-Jamie clique had, at first, served as their sanctuary from external pressure. By slow degrees it became a protection network in a more positive sense. One of Jamie's greatest battles was with himself every morning. It wasn't a question of being downright lazy. Emerging from the happy hibernation of sleep to face a mother who couldn't care enough to get him breakfast and kids who bullied him or ignored him was a miserable business. Not surprisingly, therefore, Jamie was usually late, leaving Paul without his mate. So Paul began to call for him in the mornings which meant suffering, as we had to, the long cold waits on the landing, hammering on the door, shouting through the letterbox. But it made getting up and out that much more tolerable for Jamie. He, in turn, was experiencing, for the first time in years, actual friendship. With that confidence he was rapidly perfecting his India-rubber Man act. Teasing Jamie got boring because nothing happened. Under attack he quietly withdrew into his own heavily fortified mental world leaving nothing worth the insult. And Paul needed that kind of self-defence badly. He was the ideal target for teasing and incitement to idiocy. At first Jamie accepted the role of passive sidekick in Paul's routine hysterics. Slowly his role changed. At the end of a violent scene when Paul was sitting crouched on the stairs refusing to move, to give up the scissors with which he had been going to carve up Pete for daring to touch him, Jamie could be the only person able to move him, just by being himself, cracking silly jokes until Paul was forced to laugh himself out of his corner. His motive for saving Paul from himself was probably no more or less selfish than Paul's for collecting him in the mornings — namely that he hated conflict. The results were no less beneficial for that. As Mike's paranoia about adult pressure receded, he became more likely to use his clique to pursue his scientific curiosity in ways that were constructive rather than destructive to the Centre. We were allowed to join in experiments without being suspected of trying to stop them. Other kids were pulled in. In a quiet persuasive way it became a source of security for kids and staff to know that, whatever other traumas might be going on in other corners of the Centre, those three lunatics would carry on regardless with their Heath-Robinson-like creations.

By contrast it often seemed that Tony, Jane and Christine continued to be outsiders to the group neither benefiting from nor contributing to the involvements of the others. It certainly looked like that. In an average lunch-hour there would be Sylve and Fran shrieking at each other over who had lent whom the Elvis poster, Mike, Paul and Jamie testing the explosive capacity of glue, lighter fuel and old socks, A.J. and Sam testing tolerance levels in our neighbours. By contrast, in odd corners, Tony would be talking quietly to Pete about the merits of progressive rock, Jane adjusting her make-up or discussing clothes with Ange, and Christine staring out of the window at the whole of London, imagining herself tramping the streets of Manchester in search of her mother. If the whole group was called together for an inquisition on who had broken the classroom window, nicked three quid from Ange's purse, or poured red paint into Paul's new shoes, those three said nothing and looked determinedly vacant, wishing simply that they weren't there.

Despite such appearances, these loners, in their own covert ways, had already become part of the group. Tony, at a loose end, would listen in to Fran and Sylve's hilarious dialogues. By laughing at them, teasing them gently, he made it difficult for them to keep their pose of desperate urgency. In the middle of screaming at him to get lost they would begin to laugh too. For maths, Tony had Mike to contend with, Mike, who could be brilliant in the subject, but usually sabotaged his own enjoyment by reading *Beano* under the desk. Tony's scorching contempt for Mike's 'childishness' had much more effect on Mike than anything we said.

Sometimes Tony said nothing at all. Just being there was all that mattered. Playing football was generally beneath him and if he did play, the last thing he could tolerate was pathetic rows over late tackles and missed passes. A.J., the world's greatest unrecognised soccer genius, would trail off in mid-tirade just knowing that Tony was standing behind him getting angry. It wasn't a question of charismatic personality. Quite simply Tony was bigger than anyone else and had a reputation for violent outbursts. Never once did he have to demonstrate his temper. It was enough that the other kids knew it and recognised it.

Jane had no such power. Her virtues were by local standards, prize targets for ridicule. She didn't steal, swear or smoke, she didn't fight, she couldn't parade 'flash' boyfriends. She wasn't even clever. Yet she bounced in every morning all tarted up, making out she was terribly grown up, sucking up to the teachers. A right stuck-up goody-goody — zero-rating, in fact. Of course, she suffered for it. But she couldn't be beaten and forgotten. Slowly the other kids had to admit that, underneath, she was tougher than most of them. When she was dropped off home at the end of an outing the kids made the amazing discovery that she lived in a dossy old council flat just like any of theirs. It gave them an ideal opportunity to cruficy her for her airs and graces, but the barrage of abuse never materialised. The kids were confused. Much as they resented her, they had to give her recognition for her achievement: that she could walk out of that depressing flat every day looking as if she had just been on a shopping spree in Oxford Street. She didn't produce miraculous transformations by her shining example. There was no sudden increase in smartness or saintliness. The feeling towards her always remained ambivalent, but she too was not without influence. Watching her day by day made Sylve and Fran feel that much more tatty, loud-mouthed and undesirable, and more aware of how they looked to outsiders. Worse still, Sylve and Fran found that, in their savage scramble to claim Christine a special friend, they had effectively cancelled each other out, leaving Jane free to claim the victory. For a time, Jane and Christine enjoyed their own intense womanly clique: shopping together down Chapel Market, sharing sympathy over their family responsibilities. The Terrible Twins had to sit on the sidelines, wondering why they could never keep friends. Once in a while there was direct contact. On the journey home from a trip to Wales, Jane and Sylve found themselves together in the much disputed front seat of the van. After thirty kilometres and four hundred and twenty-seven 'fucks' from Sylve, Jane bet her she couldn't stop swearing for the rest of the journey. Sylve retaliated by betting Jane she couldn't stop biting her lip (an equally repetitive habit). It was a fair match. They both won and there was a noticeable dip in Sylve's swear-count over the following weeks. That bizarre contest remained in the Centre's mythology for many months to come.

Lights and sausage dogs

I said see yer to my mates who were on the wall outside Blythe Mansions it was about 2 o'clock in the morning Sunday morning the church bells struck out the hour you could hear the bells very clearly in Hornsey Rise as if the church was just around the next corner it was getting chilly as I walked past Ashley Road where me and my mates used to go to the slags hostel last winter, and spend hours trying to get hold of a bit. I looked up in the trees, the branches were moving as if any second they would come down and try to grab me, the thing that scared me most was they were moving but there was no wind, I wished I stayed on the wall outside Blythe with my mates. I was just passing the greater London maternity hospital in Hanley Road, I looked up into the gloomy windows and suddenly the rooms

*inside lit up with sparkling jewels all shapes and sizes and colour I
stood looking up at them for a few seconds then I moved on because
a bill car was coming up the road from the Hornsey end . . . .*

Sam

5 The staff — referees or reference points?

Of course, I must be lying again. In the way I've been describing the kids' tangled involvements with each other I must seem to imply that we were there simply as note-taking observers — which we weren't. Our jobs would have been so much less agonising if we had been. But the distortion is deliberate. Whatever we may actually have been doing in the Centre's first year of life, much of the time we *felt* like observers. We were pushed into the game as referees, line-judges, first aid team and rule-makers and had to pretend that we were experts in all those roles. Behind our necessary front of self-assurance we were frequently in a state of bewilderment which stopped just short of pure panic: we didn't understand the game being played or its rules or when to treat players as injured or finally whether it was a game worth playing at all. The only thing we were even partially certain about was where the touchlines were.

I'm not bemoaning the fact. Accidentally (perhaps) it was as it should have been. Our gross naiveté prevented us from imposing a preconceived plan of events on the kids. Watching, we began to understand how much benefit the kids derived from relating to one another, that stepping aside to allow them the right to run into their own brick walls was often far more productive partly because it was more painful — for them and for us. We could see that protective intervention would often teach all of us a lot less. What I'm saying now, and what we said then is, as a basic statement of philosophy, stunningly unoriginal: we must accept people as they are — good, bad and awful. Very true, very trite and very unhelpful when you come to try and do it. It was easy enough to accept the kids for themselves in incidents such as Jane and Sylve's bet in the van — being themselves brought them into minor good-natured collision. Neither side got hurt, both sides won. But even in that story, I fiddled the facts a little. The bet had started as a one-way affair: Jane criticising Sylve. I had been driver that afternoon and was watching the exchange out of the corner of my eye. When I saw that the pressure was one-way I had suggested the reply bet to Sylve, to even the score and prop up her self-esteem a little.

Nor did we leave Tony to play out his role unprompted either.

When the opportunity arose we manipulated events there too, pushing Tony forward to stabilise potentially explosive football games, to calm Mike down to a state of concentration. We could be charged, perhaps, with cynically breaking our Golden Rule of non-intervention just in those few examples of string-pulling. But there was a more serious question than that — what did accepting people as they were mean when it was a question of accepting the unequivocally evil? If what it meant was standing back to allow A.J. to torture Jamie with razor-sharp malice then we simply weren't believers. So then we had Golden Rule Number Two: Do whatever you want as long as you don't hurt anybody. Another infuriatingly unhelpful adage. There's nothing like practice for destroying the theory. Practice is people, particular people. If this book is to mean anything, it must be about particular people, whole people — not merely their symptoms, their crises or their social disabilities. So it's appropriate that I can find no better way of describing the hellish confusions of practice than by telling the story of certain kids — even if it means breaking the chronological account.

The kids I've chosen are not intended as examples of anything. A.J. is an example of A.J., Sylve an example of Sylve. What they have in common is that they are extreme people. In their different ways they both drove us to the boundaries of sanity, self-doubt and tolerance. Insofar as they 'fit' anywhere, they fit into the Centre's history as a winner and a loser. Which was which is still very hard to say.

A.J.

No other name would have done. It had to be A.J., not Andrew or Andy. Historically, I think the name arose for no more surprising reason than that his father had the same name, but for A.J. it was always kept clouded in tantalising secrecy — A.J.: the loner, man of mystery, leader of the pack, king. It still says so all over the Centre in obscure places where we haven't repainted and all over Hornsey Rise where we can't repaint. He arrived on our second day as Andrew — small, rather pretty, charming, quiet, sensitive-looking. He just watched carefully for his first few days. In his long first day's diary entry he wrote: 'Jimmy likes to think he's tough — a bit flash. But he's OK.' We had only just reached that conclusion ourselves. Perhaps we should have worked him out more quickly, but if we had, we wouldn't have done justice to the complications of his character.

Illiterate, impatient, prone to wild fits of temper, sly, spiteful, manipulative, criminal — your actual yob. In the three and a half years we've known him, he's made a major contribution to the North London crime figures: receiving, breaking and entering, threatening behaviour, taking and driving away, and malicious wounding. Definitely he should have been put away. But he wasn't, he was with us. And on the face of it the only thing that he was when we took him that he isn't now is illiterate. It's difficult to say anything positive about A.J. without sounding like one of those naively optimistic court reports that confirms the police view of social workers as wet fools who find a broken home or sick Granny behind every delinquent and psychopath in existence. If we tried to tell those tired gentlemen at Hornsey Road Police Station that actually A.J. was a sensitive, idealistic lad they would laugh all the way to the previous convictions file.

But he was, and beneath his current attempts to be Godfather of N19, probably still is. What makes A.J. such a fascinating and crucial person to look at is the way in which the apparent contradictions in his personality interlink. To explain his behaviour by saying he is basically a 'nice boy' led astray and corrupted because of a certain character weakness by a bad neighbourhood isn't fair, and, more important, doesn't make sense. Yet the wilder the oscillations between good and bad became, the more painful it was to try to hold the idea of A.J. as a single person, to care for and hate that one person. Much easier to split up the extremes, offload our hatred and guilt on to some social devil.

There had to be something badly wrong in A.J.'s family past: he had to be at the centre of any social grouping, to be the one who controlled, the king; he wanted desperately to be approved of by adults, the men in particular, but remained deeply mistrustful, paranoid even, about anything they might try to do for him. If the group was not as happy as he'd hoped, his writing not as perfect, his picture not as neat, it hurt him so much he had to destroy it. For some eight or nine months I tried to get inside the family, but every time I got anywhere near an honest conversation, the encounter would be covertly sabotaged, either by some bland deflection from the parents (no, father and son got on perfectly well, always had done, etc.) or by the creation of a destructive misunderstanding — whatever I said to his father somehow became twisted into a betrayal of A.J.'s trust. Plainly, A.J. didn't want me looking beyond him for answers: he was demanding to be treated as himself alone. I gave up. You must start where people let you start, not according to the social work textbook.

Meanwhile, A.J. worked hard and cleverly on his status in the Centre. In the battle for leadership with Jimmy, his superior social skills slowly began to tell. From a phase when they took it in turns (quite obviously and dramatically) to be the bad guys — one week Jimmy making all the positive suggestions, encouraging participation while A.J. worked to subvert the group against us, next week total reverse — it slowly emerged that A.J. understood far more about the social dynamics of the game. Having tested out all the limits, he was able to read a look or a tone of voice as the signal for a change of tactics. When the lighting-fags-under-the-desk-in-lessons game began to lose its usefulness, he was the first to opt out, leaving the boys he'd got involved in the game to carry on to the big trouble stage. In extra-clever moments he would even encourage them to stop, thereby winning back his popularity with the staff. When new kids started he would immediately assess their strengths and weaknesses, then work hard to exploit his assessment by becoming their special friend and protector. The motives might have appeared insidious enough but the results often weren't. In practice it meant that at least three or four boys owed their easy acceptance into the Centre to A.J. He would call for them in the morning, find them and coax (or bully) them back if they went missing, warn off other kids who started to pick on them. When he was up, he could drag, manipulate and bully the whole group up with him to maintain his happy family dream of the Centre. After an exhilarating mountain-climb in Wales, the mood was threatened by the usual argument about who got the front seat for the drive home. We sat and watched A.J. transform the scene by suggesting Christine, a quiet, popular girl, as candidate for the disputed place. When he was down and saw the staff as just as uncaring and treacherous as he felt his parents to be — big trouble. Different Wales trip, same seat, same boy. We'd been to a gangster film and A.J. floated out as Robert Redford, charming, smart, the king — to find that he couldn't have the front seat. It was too painful a bring-down to bear. He fought, kicked, cried his way into the back seat, and that night instigated a long, tedious, expensive string of dormitory lunacies to pay us back for his humiliation, for smashing up his dream. Incidents like that multiplied in dozens, good and bad, always the same skill at work, the same subtle appreciation of other people's characters. The motivation remained constant — to take everyone with him in his dreams, good and bad. For a long middle period in his Centre career, A.J. was the key figure. Get him with us and we had them all. Against us, he created a united front of dissidence. He was always first to arrive in the morning; it was his Centre. Loyalty like that demands respect. We owed a lot to A.J.

It affected A.J. not a little when Jimmy lost the battle. They had been playing the same game. He was even able, with the benevolence of the victor, to offer Jimmy help. He tried to persuade us to take Jimmy back. But he also took great care not to repeat his mistakes in

losing popularity through over-use of power. His own eventual loss of
unique status was not essentially a matter of mistakes. He lost face
many times: becoming hysterical when he lost games; crying mis-
erably on the river bank, curled up in a foetal ball, when he found he
couldn't canoe as well as the others. The other kids saw through his
charisma and often kindly pretended they hadn't noticed. Of course,
A.J. would have half-killed anyone who showed him up but that
alone doesn't explain the kindness. There *was* a slowly gathering
undercurrent of resentment: 'He's all mouth, who does he think he
is, he's got no right to tell us what to do'. More, it was just that the
other kids grew up, got stronger, could cope with more flexible
variations in the grouping. They didn't need A.J. any more to be
king. The weak whom previously he'd bullied with ease, broke the
influence. In his last term, at the end of a spate of heinous crimes,
some of which had been directed against the Centre, we took him to
the police for stealing our residents' stereo. He came back (lucky as
usual, he hadn't been charged) expecting waves of admiration for his
cool brilliance. Instead he faced a largely silent Centre meeting and
worst of all, Lizzie, our smallest girl, the baby of the Centre, telling
him she was glad he'd been busted — it was right.

It's not easy to be rational and objective about someone who, in
six months, gets caught five times for stealing cars, runs to you for
help, takes without thanks, pours abuse on you if you can't give
enough, steals your tape-recorder twice, merely hates you for
catching him, accepts several periods of being looked after at the
Centre by the resident staff when he is out of home, and rewards
them by stealing everything of value they possess including their
record player, and on top of it all seems to escape any just
retribution each time with no apparent feelings except that he really
is too clever for everyone. If you get close enough to care, you're
close enough to be deeply hurt. A great deal of the time we just
wanted to beat the living daylights out of him for hurting us so much
and so callously.

We did try to think theory though. Perhaps it was anger and fear at
having reached leaving age when the Centre would have to reject
him? Was he going through a suicide act to punish us into caring?
Personally, I like that theory. At least it meant he did care about us.
And it contained an element of truth, I think, even if it was
unprovable — A.J. was the worst possible subject for the analysis
game. Having failed to be everlasting king in the Centre he had to
prove his leadership in the one obvious sphere of activity outside the
Centre — crime. The attraction of crime for A.J. was enormous. It
gave him the chance to prove himself smart and invulnerable to all

the pressures of adults with their demands which he feared so much. We could literally see the truth in that theory. A.J.'s face changed, hardened. We watched him deliberately resisting and evading the attraction of being trusted and liked, included in our relationships. He often stayed away from the Centre in his attempt to prove he didn't need us. But how long we could force ourselves to keep after him, offering friendship, soaking up his punishment, was another matter. It wasn't just a question of our stamina. Entangled in our desires for revenge was a real doubt that he might only finally learn to trust and work within the imperfect realities of living by actual rejection. We wondered how much we were, in fact, bolstering up his fantasies of a return to the unlimited, unquestioning love of early childhood by refusing to act out our anger. We argued fiercely for three solid hours over whether to take him to the police for stealing the stereo, and the person who argued most strongly against doing so was the person who'd lost the stereo.

It would be satisfying to pretend that taking him to the police and the subsequent Centre meeting changed him, but the evidence is inconclusive. Certainly his crime spree seemed to peter out (that is, he wasn't caught again for some time) and his last Centre holiday, complete with the usual confrontation (a very productive one on this occasion) brought him back into the group more as just another member than as deposed king. But when it came to actually leaving he showed that he was still capable of taking the centre of the stage. There was argument about where we should hold the end of term party. A.J. had it all planned. His parents had been pushed off to the pub for the evening well in advance. The party went to his flat, and it became his party —A.J.'s big farewell to the fans. He has even kept in more-or-less regular work since, but the grapevine rumour that says he's going around with a crowd of trainee heavies and taking a gurkha knife to someone in a pub is typical of the old A.J. temper. So there is no clear answer.

One of the most recurrent accusations levelled against the 'free school movement' is that it allows mob-rule, weakest to the wall, domination by the smartest and nastiest. What the accusation leaves out is that the smartest are also often the most socially helpful, the nicest even. In retrospect I can't feel that A.J. did any harm to the other kids in the group. At least three of the kids — Janet, Sam, Mike — would still argue long after they have grown out of his game, that they owed the start of their success in the Centre to him. What I do wonder is how much we may have harmed A.J. by using him as we did, to hold our group together. But how far you should use what is there and how far attempt to break it down to rebuild something stronger so often remains an unanswered question. A.J. both won and lost his battle to control the Centre. Perhaps we were the losers in that we never finally succeeded in getting him to see friendship except in terms of winning and losing.

Sylve: a suitable case for treatment

Sylve and her family are what you might call a classic case: a veritable adventure playground for jaded psychoanalysts. You name it, they've got it. Phantom pregnancies, broken marriages, stealing for love, illegitimate offspring, children in care, pathological lying, rampant sexual fantasy — there's a page and more of it. Their house is a true reflection of what they all feel inside. It looks as though someone has gone through the building tossing hand grenades into every room. If you arrive at half-past nine in the morning you will find a daughter asleep on the sofa, another wandering round in a dressing gown, Sylve picking through a vast pile of anybody's clothes to find something to wear, Mum pouring weak tea into a dirty mug for her two-year-old grand-daughter and a non-stop screaming match between all of them. It's normal. The household runs on extremes: an average week may contain at least one miscarriage, one running away from home, one uncle dying of incurable lung-cancer, four minor accidents and a few bonus fantasies to confuse the issue still further. There are no prizes for a correct diagnosis. Put simply, it's a family which can never love itself enough. Its members are caught in a seemingly endless oscillation between clinging desperately together for reassurance and rejecting one another completely for their failure to provide it. Always in the process of destruction but never destroyed — they cannot bear to live together but cannot survive apart either.

In retrospect our initial criteria for referrals looks a little naive, but amongst our stipulations was the requirement that the family should be stable enough to make ongoing work with the home a productive exercise. Our definition of the word 'stable' has, with experience, become much less dogmatic. We remain, however, very aware of the dangers of providing a temporary anaesthetic in situations where children would be happier if removed from home altogether.

Sylve was one of our first batch of referrals. Green as we were, it was obvious to us that the home was anything but stable. The hysterical swings from love to hate, the wild fantasies that enveloped the entire household, the screaming level of daily life: there was nothing constant for Sylve, or anyone else in the family to hold on to. All the pain and fear were registered in her eyes. Sylve was either shouting abuse, clinging desperately round our necks, or sunk in a mesmerised state of infantile withdrawal. Her soul was never at peace. We wanted a group of five; we only had seven referrals to choose from. We took her. Her elder brother Alan was one of the two whom we didn't take. We split the risks and in so doing eased our consciences somewhat. Sylve came to us. Alan went to boarding school. That decision gave us the chance for direct comparison which makes it important to look at what happened to Sylve.

Some ten or eleven months separated Alan and Sylve. They had always been very close. They had bunked off together, lied, stolen, run away from home together. If any simple statement can be made about the family, it might be fair to suggest that Alan was more favoured by Mother than Sylve. But in most other respects they had the same sufferings and the same needs. Alan's boarding-school career turned out to be a very expensive, time-consuming and largely wasted exercise, which lasted, in all, about eighteen months. The family fantasy that he would be happier away from home was too threatening to last long. One visit, after eight weeks, from Mother and Sylve and he began running. From then on it was business as usual. Alan ran home, the school was bad, Alan was protected from the police, Alan was bad, Alan went back to Stamford House, new boarding school — a good one, Alan ran again, and so on. Given the family need to split off, reject, build fantasy enemies, it was a perfect arrangement. The schools were always too far away for any productive clashes between fantasy and fact to arise. There was always a supply of new workers to love and reject in turn. Alan could enjoy the attention of his dramatic escaped-convict role at home. The police were always on hand to provide an easy exit from essential conflict, an exit which begged all the relevant questions. There were few signs, when it was at last decided to leave him at home, that he had matured at all.

It became obvious after a few days, to staff and kids alike, that Sylve was mad. With their usual appreciation of the subtleties of behaviour, the kids told her so. We squirmed in horror at their callousness until we realised that it might be the right thing to do. It gave Sylve a positive status in the group. At school she had only achieved negative status: as dirty, late, a truant, a liar, a thief, a nuisance. At the Centre Jimmy was flash, A.J. was king and Sylve was mad. It demanded, naturally enough, considerable tolerance from the group to allow her to play out the role: she broke all the normal rules about stealing, she lied when it wasn't remotely necessary, she picked up the Lady Mayor's chain of office, asked her what 'the fucking thing' was and showed them all up. She collected all the resulting abuse but, in the end, she still belonged.

It was a start. Belonging was something new to her and she couldn't take it. Being cared about and forgiven on a consistent basis was alien to her family. Love always meant rejection as well, being forgiven meant manipulation, some form of emotional blackmail. So Sylve feared it as much as she needed it. The greater the care, the worse the inevitable rejection would be. The times when care for her was most evident were the moments when she felt most compelled to seek rejection by breaking the limits of the relationship. At the end of a close, happy afternoon's cooking with the girls, Ange's purse was gone. On the day we told the group that they would not be compelled to return to school, that they were 'safe', Sylve walked into the Centre with Alan and walked out with the complete cash-box drawer. It would have been difficult enough for her to cope with being forgiven if it had only required a battle with her own self-hate and fantasy. As it was she could no more detach herself from her family's nightmare of double-binds than Alan could from the distance of a south-coast boarding school. The demands of the Centre added another to that list of double-binds. To keep love at the Centre meant breaking the conditions for acceptance in the home and vice-versa. By continuing to care in spite of what we all knew, by picking her fantasies to pieces, demonstrating how far her behaviour cut her off from friendship, we increased her pain. It was her whole family life we were dissecting so lovingly. Each time we succeeded in building up a stable place for Sylve at the Centre and she began to seem more in touch with life around her, she broke it, retreating into her home cocoon for a time. When she came back, she was high, hysterical or withdrawn in a miserable dream. Either way she was at a great distance from us again and we were back at square one. At regular intervals we decided that it was pointless trying to work with Sylve any longer. It was not simply that she seemed lost beyond recovery. We were questioning the whole morality of our mission, whether we had the right to destroy her family-centred lifestyle, desperate as it was, without the certainty that we could guarantee her a successful alternative. I began to realise for the first time the arrogance of social work intervention which fails to consider that offering a new solution to problems can mean the destruction of an existing family solution.

We carried on, often more out of sheer bloody-mindedness than from the desire to work through any optimistically-conceived case-work plan. The pattern was always roughly the same. Pressure at the Centre from staff or kids, some kind, some cruel, and Sylve would go home having been raped by one of the teachers, molested by three black men *en route*, beaten up by the kids, accused of having rabies — and Mother believed her. A routine began: first no one at home would even talk to us. As we persisted the message changed to a string of excuses as to why we couldn't talk to Mother or Sylve. There followed a delicate phase where credibility was gradually withdrawn from the initial fantasy, while we gently insisted upon our version of the facts. We still had a last stage to go through before Sylve came back — a period when Mother wanted her to return but Sylve was against us or had to look after cousin/nephew/dying uncle.

We have never seen dramatic change as a result of the necessary expenditure of time and patience, but the simple fact of belonging to a group for so long is a major part of the change for Sylve. To have survived three and a half years with the same people without rejection creates a security she has never known before. The jokes about Sylve's stories and her endless string of accidents and injuries have gone on so long that she can see them as a measure of how far she has been accepted for who she is — complete with contradictions. Now, instead of arriving each day at the Centre totally immersed in the current home drama, she arrives to tell the story plus her own interpretation of events. When, for the eighty-second time a brief period of calm at home has been broken by her mother's taking in some new family crisis — an orphaned cousin, deserted wife, dying brother — Sylve will reflect sadly that her mother seems to need the crisis to survive. Watching her sisters repeatedly leaving and returning, usually pregnant, she can discuss how difficult it is to really leave home and mean it.

There are no miracles. But Sylve is a stronger, calmer person than she was — or than she would be, had she been, like Alan, removed completely from home. Only by a long process of painful comparison, keeping both sides of her life, Centre and home, in close juxtaposition, has any change been possible. Removal from home would have frozen the process of dialogue and gradual reappraisal between her family's view of reality and her own insights as a member of an outside group. She would have been able, like Alan, to split off the conflicting parts of her response, into self-contained fantasies about how happy home was, how bad it was; it would have been very difficult indeed for her to trust any adult completely since few, if any, of those who worked with her would be able to see and accept both halves of her life.

The other kids did more than tolerate Sylve. There were times when they positively cared for her and protected her, to a far greater extent than the adult communities with which she regularly collided. But there were also times when she came perilously close to becoming prize proof of the weakest-to-the-wall doctrine. When A.J. stopped collecting Sylve on his way to the Centre each morning, he took great pleasure in announcing to the assembled company that Sylve had green teeth. She was fair game. Feeling understandably hurt by Sylve's endless double-crossing and lies, Fran was more than once

poised for the kill. Fran's family Mafia had to be hauled off the hunt.
We had to plead Sylve's special case, invoke an ideal of forgiveness
which came very close to implying that she was less than a whole
person.

Removing kids like Sylve from the multiple tortures of their homes
to the clean safety of residential care can look like winning — to the
police, to the neighbours, to guilt-ridden social workers. We have
nothing so decisive as victory to claim by having kept Sylve out of
Care. But having had her wild laughter, crazy jokes and manic games
booming round the Centre for three years feels much more like
winning than losing.

Linda and Kathy

The front door bangs open and in runs Linda and Kathy.
They say:
'Doreen, is Daddy in?'
and I say:
'No — where do you think you're going?'
Linda says:
'You mind your own business!'
I say:
'You better shut your bloody mouth before I come out and shut it
for you!'
'Oh shut up,' *Linda would say;* 'Kathy, come on.' *They both walk
into the kitchen and I hear a lot of banging around in there,*
and I say:
'Where you going?',
and Linda or Kathy would say:
'We're going swimming',
and I say:
'Did Daddy say you can go?'
and Kathy says:
'We can't find him',
and I say:
'Be back before Dad gets in!'

   Doreen

'Call yourselves teachers?'

'We do more work here than you do and you get paid for it and we
don't. We do all the painting round the place and all the woodwork

and you just stand round and supervise. We are the ones who do all
the writing — you don't.'

A.J.

We couldn't have been of much use to A.J., Sylve or any of the other
kids if they had only been able to see us as teachers — albeit
super-friendly ones. We had actually as well as symbolically forfeited
our claim on super-teacher roles when we let the 'Sir' and 'Miss'
routine go. But if we weren't teachers we couldn't claim with any
honesty to be friends either. Of some things the kids were quite sure:
we were there because we were paid to be, we were there to teach
and to hold power. When Carol came to replace Sally, our art
teacher, and tried to sell herself to the girls *simply* as a matey big
sister, she was greeted with scorn and suspicion. But within the broad
limits set by the kids as to how we should respond to them, there was
a large space to be filled. Behind the questions of when to intervene,
when to stand back, whether to be referee or reference point, lay the
prime issue of who to be in relation to the kids, how far to let them
decide our roles, how far to insist that we were ourselves.

At the outset we imagined that we were presenting ourselves as
three individuals to whom the kids could relate as they wished. We
claimed, when questioned, that we had no leader, no labels, were all
equal, doing the same job. I don't know why we bothered. Whatever
we said, the kids were in no doubt. As a team consisting of a married
couple plus one it was predictable enough: mother, father and big
brother/uncle. Long after the cosy family atmosphere of the first
four months had evaporated those broad outline roles remained in
force. Our personalities and behaviour were frequently and obviously
at odds with our assigned positions, but that didn't reduce the
usefulness of the myth as a structure within which we could all work.
In times of crisis all three of us disappeared for a council of war in
the office. What emerged was, in our view, a joint decision of the
triumvirate. As far as the kids were concerned it was emphatically
my decision. Pete, in his most confident mood, laying down the law
on any issue, still had to put up with 'What does Rob say?' Ange
could be as tough and unbending as any stereotype dad. It didn't
stop the kids turning naturally to her as mediator and sympathiser.

No two kids carry the same family in their heads. For our first five
we had to be simultaneously five different sets of parents and uncles.
A.J.'s mum was putty in his hands, to be treated with ingratiating
cunning and contempt. He didn't trust his dad further than he
wished he could throw him. So Ange was a real problem. The
Oscar-winning wide-eyed-little-boy routine didn't deliver the goods.
Withering contempt wasn't much use as a face-saver when she had

just dumped him out on the front doorstep. Since he couldn't get between the two of us as he could with his own parents, she was worse than a wash-out as go-between. So Pete got the job instead, and kept it even when our latter-day Macchiavelli began to realise that messages sent via Pete only meant that he ended up facing both of us taking the same line.

Pete had a less easy job when it came to Paul and Fran. Dads might be dangerous, mums two-faced but at least they were family. Pete's crime was not being family. 'Fuck off you. You can't order us around. You don't run this place. You just make trouble.' With that beard and those 'hippy clothes', he had to be cast as an outsider, a saboteur. If I moved in to support his judgement it was 'You're just sucking up to Rob 'cos you're too weak to stand up for yourself'. A heads-we-win, tails-you-lose part. At least in Sylve's fantasy he could claim a positive vice — that of being a wicked marriage-busting sex-maniac. 'Rob, your wife's alone in the office with that Peter Davis. Oi, get off, you dirty old man. I can see you.' But it was an honour equally shared by all three of us. 'Ange, where were *you* this afternoon? *We* know.' 'Ange, I saw Rob down the Nag's Head with a blonde.' Now and again we got the real fear: 'Are you two ever going to get divorced?'

However exhausting it became having to be a troupe of quick-change artistes, we had to recognise that the casting was necessary. Without it we would be, in the kids' eyes, nobody — nobody they knew. Outside the Centre and home, everyone had a known and agreed status. Teachers were there to tell you things in classrooms; they could bore you, be teased by you, clobber you, but only on school territory. Social workers were suckers, nosey bastards, two-faced, but powerless outside of court. And the Old Bill were real bastards who could clobber you anytime, for anything. We were not, categorically, any of those people, but a weird amalgam: teachers who poked their noses in their homes, social workers who taught lessons, adults you could say 'Fuck off' to but who reserved the right to throw you out just the same. It would have been meaningless and dangerous to stand, radiating love for humanity, saying, 'Hello, kids, here we are, just three individuals, like yourselves, holding out our hands to you'. The response would have been, quite properly that we were 'a right bunch of idiots'. As it was, the kids were astute judges of character and our parts fitted well. Whether I liked it or not (and listening to my own voice as I roared orders down the stairs, I frequently didn't) I was rightly cast as father-figure. Naturally, I hid my fears behind dogma and fake self-assurance, and they believed me. Ange was tough and maternal. Pete was, by nature, the easy-going middle-man, a pragmatist. As a starting-point it was good, but not good enough for the kids, or for us. If we remained walking projections of their real or fantasy parents, we could get them no further than they had already got with fourteen years of the same. We could hardly expect them to accept themselves as confused whole people without demanding that they should accept us in the same way. Of course, we knew who we really were and they didn't (or so we said). We knew what the game should be. But, to misquote Bob Dylan, it was a case of 'I'll let you be in my game, if I can be in yours'. Clearly, we needed a working compromise. The trouble was that while each different game may have had its own rules, there were no ready-made rules for the new in-between game.

The post-lunch hiatus. It was always a critical moment with the safe bit of the day — the morning lessons — over, and the uncertainty of afternoon activities yet to come. The kids rarely listened to or absorbed what we told them about the plans for the week. So, for them, it was a guessing game which could generate a lethally high mood. It was necessary, therefore, if tedious, to keep a constant message running to all the kids until they had all been reassured about what we were doing. No plan was foolproof: it rained, the van broke down, the museum or exhibition was closed, and we would be left with an empty space to fill. Theoretically, the answer was to discuss possible alternatives in an open meeting with the kids. Practically, that answer was usually suicidal. The anxiety raised by having the possibility of choice thrown at them produced wild enthusiasm followed by a chaos of conflicting impossible suggestions — an afternoon in France, a helicopter trip round London, a tour of the strip-clubs — followed swiftly by collapse into depression.

The tactic which worked was the brutal opposite: a lightning staff meeting in the secrecy of the office, an arbitrary decision and a whirlwind drive down through the Centre to cajole, bully, and carry all the kids out on the trip. 'You'll never know whether you like it till you try. I don't give a damn what you think. Stop yapping. Just *move*.' That's what the kids wanted, and it was awful. Just about everything we didn't believe in. It left the kids without the right of choice or the chance to practise the skill of choosing from what was possible, recognising for themselves what was impossible. It left them free to moan, quite legitimately, about whatever we did since they hadn't chosen it. Responsibility was firmly on us. The myth that power always lies elsewhere lived to crush another day. We found ourselves mimicking that old colonialist argument, 'Of course, we believe in self-government — ultimately. The present policy is merely an expedient because the natives aren't ready for such responsibility yet'. If we didn't believe them, there was little reason to believe ourselves. How did we have the right to make godlike decisions? Did we have the strength to ensure that the expedient didn't become permanent?

Within the group, with each kid the same dilemmas arose again and again. At least in the example I've just given we could claim that it worked: having bullied Fran into venturing out of the womb of N19 to see the boring old Cutty Sark, we could watch her racing along the river bank, saying she'd never seen the Thames before and when could we go on a boat-trip? Playing individual games so often seemed sterile and counter-productive. Little brother Paul told A.J. he beat up two 'Pakis' round his flats with one hand behind his back. A.J. smartly spotted the chance for a giggle and made the obvious challenge. Thirty seconds into the fight Paul discovered what we could have told him earlier but deliberately hadn't; that he should learn to keep his mouth shut and his fantasies to himself. He'd been picked on, beaten up without reason, his jacket torn, his mum would be furious. Big sister Fran came squawking and flapping to the rescue. 'Call yourself bloody teachers — you're useless. You're supposed to stop fights. And you're just fucking standing there. You're chicken. Haven't got the guts to stop A.J. — the big bully.' By this time Fran was at a higher pitch of hysteria than Paul who now began to relax into acting the hapless victim sensing that, as usual, the family cavalry had come to the rescue. We had a choice then. We could have refused to intervene, let A.J. drive his advantage home with his own vicious brand of ridicule which would have left Paul feeling humiliated and desperate, and his sister full of anger at our betrayal. Or we could have stepped in and lectured them both, trying to put both sides, attacking A.J. for being nasty enough to create an obviously sadistic situation and Paul for being stupid enough to give him the chance to do it. That might not have worked either. Paul would probably have ignored the sermon and drawn the simpler conclusion that he would always be saved from himself. I can't say what we did, because this wasn't one incident but a whole number of similar incidents. What we did in each case was always different.

If I wanted neatness rather than truth I would say that we followed a predetermined plan: that we slowly changed our role from that of parent-protectors to acting more as football coaches shouting guidance from the sidelines. In truth it then seemed a hopelessly haphazard business. The time of day, the mood of the other kids, the weather, our level of tiredness were all as important as any master plan in deciding how we reacted. The only consistent thread in our thoughts was the instinct not to lose the kids' trust in us. When we were feeling strong and pushed hard on Paul and Fran, through the defensive barrage — the threats of massive family retaliation, the emotional blackmail, insults to our manhood — it was sometimes very clear that we were losing touch, that they were struggling to hold together two conflicting images. We were trusted as benevolent protectors and yet they felt us to be saying something hard and uncaring. As long as we kept in touch, held the gap between the images within their grasp, they could fight to keep themselves listening. We could say 'Fran, you're right to want to help Paul but you'll only do it by making him take the consequences of what he does'. At the end of an hour they might actually accept that we weren't, like the rest of the world, hell-bent on the destruction of their family. This doctrine of self-reliance might not be total blasphemy.

The most dramatic example of the painful art of dream-breaking involves Sylve, that most dramatic of ladies. She blew into the Centre, threw her arms round me, informed me that I was her daddy, would I marry her, had I seen the real silver ring her uncle had given her on his death-bed, did I know that her sister had had a miscarriage the night before? An hour later she was clinging to Ange's arm, screaming at Pete and I that we were dirty old men, that she had to leave early to see her uncle in hospital, that her sister's baby was due in a week. Before we had the chance to ask what we were supposed to believe, she dissolved into helpless laughter and rushed out the door with Fran to swop her Woolworths ring for two Elvis singles. Somewhere in that mad muddle we had to find someone called Sylve to whom we could really talk. Catching her out was easy enough: inconsistency was the only consistent thing about Sylve. 'You've got to leave early to see your uncle in hospital, right?' 'Yes.' 'But you told us this morning that he was dead.' 'I never. It was a different uncle.' 'You've only got one uncle, Sylve.' 'Liars, I've got three.' 'OK, supposing your uncle really is in hospital, what are the visiting hours?' 'Six to seven-thirty.' 'Fine, then you don't need to leave early.' 'Oh bollocks the lot of you, leave me *alone*!' Her face emptied of all expression, her eyes went dead, she drew up her knees and left us with nothing. Caught stealing, she would be consumed with guilt and repentance. It was real. Forgive her and it was gone. She would bubble happily around the room, pleading favours from Ange whose purse she had stolen, who reminded her gently of what she had just put us through. Total recoil. We'd lost her again by trying to put the fragments of her life together.

To get to Sylve we had to find a way of saying two things at once. My best game with her usually began with the worlds: 'It's not that I don't trust you. It's just that I don't trust you.' It was, at once, the unkindest and the most reassuring thing I could say to her, because it was honestly what I felt. Careful kindness she had had in plenty over the years, from teachers and social workers — the sort of kindness that tacitly ignored what she knew about herself: that she was a liar, a cheat, an unreliable friend. What she needed most, but feared she couldn't tolerate, was for the pretence to stop, for someone to say 'I know what you're like and will tell you to your face. But I still like you just the same.'

We were all very frightened of taking that risk. We shared a strong fantasy that if we did we would leave ourselves hopelessly vulnerable and the kids in shattered misery. My battle with Mike taught me, more than anything else, that it wasn't true.

For a start, I found it difficult to like him. He seemed sly, sneaky, evasive, undermining. He would ask for help in a maths lesson, wait till I was leaning over his shoulder enjoying being helpful, then tell me I had bad breath and push me away. He'd arrive in the office, relax us into talking about our own childhoods with a show of genuine curiosity, then tell us we talked like a load of queers and walk out. A black-belt back-stabber in fact. We understood his 'problem' well enough but that didn't make him any less unpleasant a person. He was a runner — the first we'd experienced. To our and the other kids' amazement ('What the hell are you running from? No one's going to get at you here. It's different') he would walk in the front door, out the back and run off across the garden walls as though he were a spy in East Berlin with the entire KGB on his tail. He lived in continual terror of what he thought he saw. He didn't see or hear Pete and me at all. He saw giants of male aggression closing in for the kill and tortured himself by dancing round the edge of suicide, provoking violence and running from it. He ran in the lunch-hour. I drove to his house to collect him. His mum blocked the back door and he was forced to come out to the car. I was sick to death of him, longing just to belt him round the ear for all the weeks of double-crossing and contemptuous put-downs. That's precisely what he fears, I thought, and therefore precisely what I mustn't do. He got in the car and I said nothing. 'Don't you dare shout at me' was the first thing he said.

I kept after him out of sheer pride. I was damned if this little bastard was going to reject my beautiful loving Centre. Every day I talked calmly, quietly and rationally, dodging the snide remarks, ignoring the contempt. One Thursday afternoon he was drifting around, refusing to commit himself to any activity. Everyone else in the Centre was happily involved, and Mike, as usual, was spoiling it. I spent twenty minutes talking him into cutting the front hedge with me. We started the job and he relaxed into talking about his home. Suddenly he disappeared. I stormed upstairs into the kitchen and saw him standing by the window, smirking. That was it. Walking softly up behind him, I swiped him round the head. An immensely satisfying way of ruining two months' hard work. He fled from the Centre, pouring every imaginable abuse at me, swearing he'd never come back.

I believed him. I had just succeeded in confirming his worst fears about men. I spent the weekend wondering why I'd been stupid enough to think of starting the Centre at all. Come Monday, he was there on time. To start with he was very wary, but there was no talk of big brother coming up after school to punch my head in or even bigger Mum reporting me to the Council. It was understood without words that the incident was strictly a personal matter between the two of us. The message I got from the way he acted and looked was that he was, deep down behind his defences, mightily relieved. He had got what he was asking for — an honest bit of me. He'd hit my limits and the reality had proved to be nothing like as awful as the fantasy. From that point onwards we were building up from the fact that he actually trusted me. If he was markedly more cooperative, which he was, it wasn't fear that kept him so. We'd already seen that fear produced the opposite result. In fact, Mike moved sharply from one fantasy about me — big ogre — to another — father protector. For six months he was my shadow. Everywhere I went around the Centre, Mike was half a step behind. But it wasn't just a different myth, it was a more inclusive myth. When I had to put pressure on him, there was a mutually-recognised game for including his fear about my exercise of authority: we went through a mime of violence. A quick half-nelson, he told me he'd kill me when he got free, I told him I'd knock his head off if he tried. It wasn't a position that any good liberal educator would care to be caught in. But it was a good working version of the truth of what we both felt at that moment. A year before, any teacher or social worker who had dared to put Mike in a head-lock would have seen only panic and hysteria. But then no teacher or social worker would have had the chance to earn that right of friendship. By the end of his first year, Mike and I actually liked each other.

Mike was asked to leave the Centre for the rest of the day. After mutual agreement he returned, and wrote his thoughts out on the typewriter.

Stay . . . .

I might stay, I could stay, but I don't think I'll stay, on second thoughts I will stay, then again I mightn't stay, but I think I will stay, but go now.

Go

Can I GO now?!
Yes you may GO!
But I don't want to GO!
Then why say you wanna GO?
I didn't say I wanted to GO!
Yes you did say you wanted to GO!
I refuse to GO!
But I don't want you to refuse to GO!
Then you don't want me to GO?!
But I do want you to GO!
Alright I will GO!
Don't GO yet!
But I want to GO!
Then GO!
Alright bye!

Mike

6 'This ain't a proper school'

It must seem perverse in the extreme to have gone so far without more than peripheral mention of one of our main functions in running the Centre — teaching. This has been deliberate. For what we discovered over the first few months (if 'discovered' is a suitable word to use about something that has been said at regular intervals for over a hundred years) was that teaching cannot meaningfully be considered apart from the teacher and the taught — their moods, their morale, their relationship to each other. Teaching is not merely a matter of appropriately timed and designed input being fed to well-tuned receivers by skilled operatives. As much, and more, good teaching depends on who is teaching whom, whether they care about and trust each other. But before all else there is one simple question: whether those receiving education believe that it holds anything useful and valuable for them.

That was precisely what our kids didn't believe. After all, they were truants. We would have been crazy to assume otherwise. We expected beforehand that the kids would be well behind the standard for their age, that they would be resistant to teaching, out of practice, depressed by their failure to learn. They rapidly proved to be all those things, and we weren't too worried by the fact. We were offering them a new deal: small groups, a high level of personal attention, friendship, and the chance of self-respect. It wasn't enough. Whatever we said to one another about the irrelevance of conventional education to the majority of kids was all unabsorbed theory. We hadn't felt what it meant.

In our second week of operation I was sitting with Fran trying to test her spelling. Having spelt 'and' wrong for the third time, she became desperate and angry with me. 'It's no bloody good *you* asking *me* the questions. There ain't nothing in my head. It's all in your head. That's your job, you're the teacher. You've got to take it out of your head and put it into mine.' It was a classic statement. At one level it was an exact expression of what she, and many of the other kids, felt at the times when every shred of self-confidence deserted them: that they had nothing at all to give, that to insist that they had merely added to the humiliation. But beyond that, it was a statement of what, in any mood, she believed education was about: the implanting of facts and answers, 'filling the empty pitchers' in true Gradgrind style.

The kind of lessons they all enjoyed most demonstrated that her belief was a shared one. What they demanded was 'chalk and talk', the more chalk the better: plenty of writing on the board, numbered points one, two and three to be copied into their books. Lessons got their value rating according to the number of pages filled. A.J. loved the copying down — it was real progress to him. Asked to explain what he had written, he felt outraged — it was a double-cross. He had achieved the aim of the lesson by writing everything down. To be told that the aim was something else, actually understanding, was a cruel deception. Sylve could go one better. She could memorise almost anything and play the answers back to us. Yet it meant no more to her than reciting three random pages from the telephone directory. She was similarly hurt by any suggestion that it mattered whether she really understood what she said. 'I said it all right, didn't I? Well then, shut your face. What more do you want?' Jimmy was smart: he'd learnt on the road with his dad. Driving all over England in a lorry, listening to his father's chat, he had picked up a sizeable assortment of geographical and general knowledge. In lessons he would use it but only to score points in the battle for leadership. The idea that he might want or be able to explore further was an invasion of his private life, which should be safe from learning. He didn't want to kill the fun and kudos of his experiences by bringing education into it. Only Paul, with his uncontainable childlike curiosity, seemed able to break through the fact that he was in lessons. When he broke the rules — that in lessons you either work to please teacher by writing things down or to please your mates by not so passive resistance — he was usually teased into suppressing his curiosity. But just occasionally, even in those early days, and weak as he was in the eyes of the group, he took the others up with him. Those ten minute flashes of real eagerness to understand kept us going.

It was easy enough to see why the losers felt that learning was a meaningless game. It was the only available method of self-defence against the humiliation of being branded as thick. Looking down at their books, the ragged patterns of lines which no one could understand as words would make A.J. and Fran frantic with anger. They would tear out page after page before we could calm them down. The difference between the perfect dream in their heads and what appeared on the page was too crippling to be tolerated. The frustration had been grinding them down further and further over their years at school. A.J. used all his art to disguise his failures to understand: twice as much intelligence as it would have taken to grasp the problem in the first place, in theory. But in practice what he had learnt was that the learning game was a series of mysterious codes which teachers and a handful of kids were born to understand — and he wasn't. He and his fellow losers hung on to the fragments of code they had learnt as though they were magic talismans. Time after depressing time, they failed to deliver the right answers. It didn't make any difference — those fragments were all they had. They wouldn't dare to risk losing them on the wild chance that they might gain a code that worked better. Every area we probed gave us the same results, the next thing up from nothing. The beginning of the world. The position of America. Our system of government. The capital of England. Nothing. They hadn't been truant all their lives. At some time, for some years, there must have been teachers in front of them pouring out their knowledge with some degree of energy and skill. But it would have been difficult to prove; the evidence was so slight. What little there was had no purpose or place in their minds. In the middle of a lesson on the origins of Man, Fran said 'Monsters', a propos of nothing anyone had said. A breakthrough, we thought. 'Yes, Fran, what about monsters? Where do they come in?' 'How the hell do *I* know? You're the mister know-all. I just said it.'

Sylve, Jimmy, Mike — A or B stream kids who had got those magic codes — didn't have that humiliation to bear. They knew the answers, could read the words. All we had to do was to show them exciting ways to use the tools they had. But it was never that simple. Getting the answers right came easily to them but so often they found satisfaction in that and no more. It was a game they could play, a trick like balancing pennies on your nose — as clever, and as irrelevant to anything they deeply cared about in their lives.

Mike had an incurably scientific mind. He couldn't help wanting to know why things worked. On our second trip to Wales we climbed a mountain. Even the pathetic moaners made it to the top. We all collapsed for a smoke on the top, felt stunned by the view, got blown off our feet, floated frisbies out down the mountain-side. Everyone was high and happy. Half-way down the mountain Mike and Paul found a spring, and wanted an answer why. We traced how it ran, drank it, worked through the whole rain cycle. They were both totally 'there', absorbing every word. Suddenly Mike began to look suspicious, realising he'd been conned. 'This isn't lesson-time.' End of 'lesson'.

As pupils, as well as people, we had to accept the kids the way they were. What they wanted was structure and safety — neat self-contained packages of learning where we taught and they learnt. With the 'worst' kind of teaching method they felt secure: a fixed target, a fixed time-span, results they could see and measure. Copying maps from the board of places they neither knew nor cared about, the kids settled in peaceful silence. We could watch their faces relax as the anxiety died away. The anxiety was that they would be asked to give and think, when they supposed they had nothing to give or think with.

It wasn't true. At lunch they had opinions in plenty, particularly about the blacks and the Pakis. It seemed to me such an obvious place to start, so I planned out a lesson on racial attitudes — a straight survey of what they thought, with no judgements and no 'right' answers. They designed the questionnaire with me, enjoying filling in their answers. From that point on it was a disaster. The answers weren't the same. 'Was Jimmy right?', why were they wrong? I couldn't convince them, because they couldn't listen, that there were no right answers. Here, in a lesson, hating Pakis because they're 'dim' and 'chicken' was obviously wrong. They sensed what I thought, even though I hadn't said it. They had lost, as usual, and more hopelessly than usual since they could do nothing about it. My prize-winning lesson in open-ended exploratory learning produced five miserable, depressed people who spent the rest of the day refusing to get involved in activities — to get their own back for my rubbing salt in their wounds.

Our biggest source of amazement was that, as a 'proper school' the Centre worked. These champion runners from 'education' came into lessons, did what we asked of them, struggled to get the answers right, asked for exams at the end of term, even proved in doing them that they had 'learnt' something. But it wasn't the proper school that we believed in.

'Arson' was a set class exercise where it was imagined that the Centre was set on fire by Sam, and different members of the group assumed roles of real or imaginary people involved. Kathy wrote about how she imagined Rob would react.

I found out afterwards that Sam had lit the fire. I was angry and very very hurt. And however much we tried, my feelings towards Sam have changed in that knowing and trying to forget makes it difficult for me to communicate with Sam. Which is a shame because being able to talk is one of the main things that makes the Centre what it is.

I know that Sam's very emotional but I started this project and Sam knew how much it means to me.

I decided to walk up to Sam and give him a good telling off. I

*didn't know how he would react but I was very angry. When I had a
go at Sam, he closed right up. And it didn't help matters at all.*

Kathy

Troubles in translation

We became used to their forgiveness. Week by week, we taught some
bad and boring lessons for which, in a 'proper school' we would be,
quite deservedly, taken apart by our classes. Here we were pardoned,
given the chance to try again. What the kids cared most about was
having us as people to teach them. It was us they wanted, our
attention not our curriculum. 'You're not a proper teacher.' 'Why
not?' 'Well, like if we get it wrong, you go on about it like it really
mattered or something.' 'It does to me.' 'That's what I mean, you
take it personal. You're mad.' Pete was brilliant at taking it
'personal'. He became obsessed with the subject of space, came
staggering into the Centre loaded with books, diagrams, pictures,
ideas and enthusiasm. The kids thought he was mad, certainly. He
was totally convinced that they were going to be as enthusiastic as he
was. He was right: after two or three lessons it was space everywhere — moonscapes on the walls, model spaceships flying out the
windows, arguments about UFO's over lunch.

The more they trusted us as people, the more they were able to
trust us with their ignorance and long-buried curiosity and the less
they worried about education. Fran's questions always began 'I know
you'll think I'm silly but . . .'. Sitting beside me in the van on the
way back from a visit Fran had forgotten how silly she was. It had
been a warm funny day out. She began to ask. Over the twenty miles
home she asked more than thirty different questions. 'Why don't
birds fly backwards? Why can't we fly? Where does milk come from?
Who invented roads?' On and on. I couldn't keep up. Every answer
had to begin with fundamental concepts, which I assumed in
everything I thought and saw, and which she didn't possess.

We had a language problem. I don't mean the problem of long
words and complicated phrases. Nothing so superficial. What we
began to realise was that the kids didn't think about time or space or
cause and effect in the same way as we did. Perhaps that *is* a
stunningly obvious remark. If it is, then that in itself is part of the
problem. To be in our minds, using our minds to examine our minds
is so near to the impossible that it seems hardly worth the pain and
effort to try. It's much more comfortable to spend ten minutes

giving a brilliantly simplified explanation of the aerodynamics of bird flight and rage at Fran afterwards for her monolithic stupidity in failing to understand. The trouble was that none of us believed that Fran or any of the other kids *were* stupid. We had to find out why they behaved as though they were.

'When's the Centre holiday?' '15 June.' 'When's that?' 'Well it's 17 May today, we have June next after May. So it's just under a month away, isn't it?' 'How long's that, then?' 'Round about thirty days, just over four weeks.' 'So when are we going on holiday?' At which point we would reach for the nearest heavy object and only just succeed in not throwing it. Holidays were what they cared about and looked forward to, most of all. Surely they could remember *that*? But no, we would have the same idiot conversation two days later with the same pea-brained kids. When we calmed down sufficiently we would teach them the months and days of the year and they would learn the facts. It didn't make any difference. The academically 'clever' kids could be just as bad. We couldn't note it as a classic symptom of a remedial stream pupil. Their time-sense didn't operate on the same scale as ours. All their lives it had been borrowing milk from next door till tomorrow, lasting two days till the Social Security money came, surviving through Friday without getting caught by the tallyman. The maximum stretch of time to be felt about was a week. There was a shape to a week: high from Friday night through to Sunday when the wage packet got thin, a small lift on the way down with Monday's family allowance and then a long, slide down through the week, hitting the ground on Friday morning. Dates came from some inscrutable source elsewhere: the beginning of term, the holidays, days off for elections, check-ups at the dentist. All these just happened. No purpose could be served by thinking about, trying to understand them — they were beyond the range of time sense and beyond control. We got the message and then thought about the lessons we were going to do on 'London a hundred years ago'. How on earth did we start? 'Right kids, how many weeks in a hundred years?'

Space too. We'd be crossing the North Circular on the van drive to Wales we'd done three times before. 'Are we nearly there?' 'Does it feel like it?' 'Yeah, it's been hours.' Two hours later, threading through the one-way maze in Cheltenham we got treated to 'Are we still in London?' and similar choice witticisms that made us wish we'd decided to camp on Hampstead Heath instead. Fran, with her natural genius for brain-fusing questions, stood on Simmonds Yat examining the course of the River Wye below us. In the middle of the answer to her question about 'Why don't rivers run out?' she said 'Can you see London from up here?' 'No.' 'Well, I can see the moon and that must

be further away than London. So why can't I see London?'
'Because . . .'. There was no denying her logic. Distance was the trip
on the bus to Chapel Market every Saturday with the family. Dad
driving the car to Granny's and a few other familiar corridors across
London. It didn't matter, therefore, whether London was just one
place on the planet forty kilometres across, or a way of life that
covered the whole surface of the earth. If the place name had no
emotional significance, then forget it — it went on a jumbled pile
labelled 'somewhere else'. Drawing maps was always good fun and
the kids could achieve high standards on miles per hour between
London and Birmingham problems. Making up pretty patterns and
working out the time it took a policeman to fall from the top of Big
Ben could be fun too. There really wasn't much difference.

If they hadn't got a 'real' time sense or space sense . . . . On
holidays we visited amazing places. The kids were duly amazed:
castles, caves, cliffs, waterfalls, mountains up in the clouds. It
produced tremendous response. The kids were genuinely quite
alarmed to realise that clouds actually hung above our heads, could
be reached and touched. They had assumed that they were somehow
painted on the sky. That stalactites took millions of years to form
stunned them. We had to work desperately hard to catch and hold
the moments of amazement. What depressed us was that they were
only moments. If the kids were involved in discussing their criminal
records or playing cards, we could drive past anything short of little
green men in flying saucers without arousing much interest. But then
that too was logical. We, the teachers, could look at a rock formation
and become involved in thinking about the astonishing patterns of
the strata, but it was only astonishing if you knew something about
geological formation. Otherwise it was pretty and just 'there'. Rain is
wet and boring and falls out of the sky from time to time. Castles are
old and left half-demolished. Rivers are bits of water which you can't
see the ends of.

We sat in Friday meetings, agonising over the next week's timetable, saying those obvious things to each other, aware that, to the
proverbial fly on the wall, we must sound condescending. This was
the basic material for the dedicated workers in the Deprivation
Industry. These poor kids had been deprived of the normal stages of
conceptual development upon which education rests. Naturally, I'm
going to insist that we didn't think like that. Being able to write
about their language when they couldn't write about ours makes the
accusation that we were patronising almost inevitable. But it's still
true that we felt as stupid in their world as they did in ours. We
laboured around the edge of their lives, constructing theories about
the neighbourhood, the role of the caretakers in their flats, their

relationship with the police. They just knew and could dodge their way through day after day of complicated and contradictory pressure: soft-talking Mum to get money to pay off their mate who got on well with the neighbours who were going to tell the caretaker about the broken window which they hadn't done anyway but knew who had — and still finding time to 'forget' everything, and go roller-skating. We would have been on our knees by lunch-time, torn to bits by trying to 'think' about it all. Maybe its easier to convey the difference by pointing out Jamie, who was very 'deprived'. He must have been born with perfect eyesight and he survived being deprived by using it. With his mother having left that morning 'for ever' again, with noise and pressure all around him to have lunch ready in fifteen minutes, Jamie could still spend his time pondering carefully over the minute patterns in the potato he was peeling, patterns that no one else could even see. In the middle of a beach with a fight, two attempted rapes and a game of football in progress, Jamie could stand calmly in goal watching a bird diving for fish a hundred and fifty metres out to sea — beautiful for him, and invisible and infuriating for everyone else. The answer might have been to leave Jamie to get on with his world. Unfortunately, he also wanted to understand how birds dived for fish, why potatoes grew in that way — and we wanted to tell him. We wanted to tell him because we believed that he would enjoy knowing. We also felt certain that if we didn't get him to see more than the object before his miraculous eyes, that he would be steam-rollered sooner or later by the rest of humanity who didn't realise that he didn't belong in their world.

If we hadn't been able to tolerate our own arrogance in assuming that we had something of value to give the kids then we would have had no business to keep the Centre open. The problem was to find areas where the two worlds touched, where the effort of translation could be justified.

A game of chance

Planning was what was required, or so it appeared. Basic literacy and numeracy were essential, we were quite sure of that. Like it or not, they would have to live in a literate, numerate society when they left school. Without those basic skills they would be certain losers — over Social Security, rent, wages, debts, anything and everything which required a form to be filled in or money to be reckoned. The kids knew it and believed it, even if faith in their ability to reach a minimum standard often seemed too difficult to hold. Beyond that we became steadily less sure. Strong knowledge of their civil rights had to be part of any survival kit. But then — awareness of our political system, of their environment, of hygiene and food, economics, job opportunities? I could list instances of the kids rejecting every one of these burningly relevant topics: 'Who cares about politics, they're in control and that's that. So Hornsey Rise stinks. We *know*. What are you going to do — buy us all houses in the country? Bad food and all that's going to kill us? We could be run down by a bus tomorrow' — and so on. But that would be misleading. Relevance is a matter of a particular moment.

Pete wanted to talk about football violence, the social scene on the North Bank at the Arsenal ground. He had a trendy article about it which he thought was pompous and inaccurate. The kids all knew what it was really like. Pulling the article apart would get them started. It should have worked, especially since he had A.J. in the group — the self-acclaimed expert on the subject. Instead they were merely bored: 'What's the point in talking about it? We know already. If you don't, then go to the game on Saturday. Now tell us something we don't know.' But we couldn't then draw a neat conclusion about good material having to be from outside their experience. Not even when in the next lesson I had the same group for a session about living on the Moon (of all the irrelevant subjects) and a beautiful hour's worth of interest. We had fantasies about what weightlessness must feel like developing into a discussion of gravity leading to the problem of the population explosion, ending in diagrams, stories and even missing the lunch-call. The difference was in the people. In Pete's lesson, A.J. felt he was going to be criticised for his behaviour on the terraces and worked the whole group round to hostility in order to protect himself. By the time he reached my lesson he had calmed down, allowing Mike and Paul the chance to let their imaginations run without fear of being laughed at by him.

Witnessing the staggering effect of individuals and their moods on a group at work, it was difficult not to conclude that success or failure depended solely upon them. Fran, feeling undermined, could wreck a morning demanding exclusive attention, giggling in corners with Sylve, blasting all and sundry with bitter invective. When happy she might sit totally mindless for half the lesson then out of nowhere, as a bored silence fell, unleash a string of extraordinary questions which showed she had been listening all the time. A group who were beginning to get exhausted with talking about the earth's atmosphere suddenly had Fran saying: 'How do you know there's air in this room and how can it weigh anything if its invilible, invi . . . you know, that word, what you said? And shut up, you wankers, laughing bloody jackdaws. Bet you don't know.' She was right, they didn't. She could make them laugh, relax and get curious again in ten seconds — which is more than we could. Crazy Sylve was another two-faced genius in lessons: unbearable to the point of incitement to murder or capable of running the whole show single handed. Trying to talk about incidents with the police could leave the kids in abysmal depression. But if we managed to work Sylve up to acting, she would lead a doorstep drama involving neighbours, police, arguments and punch-ups — everything we had wanted to discuss and hadn't managed to.

Even kids who stood away from the main group and seemed socially powerless might still get the other kids moving. After nine or ten months most of the kids were bored with Art, except Tony who was a gifted artist and typically carried on painting, totally indifferent to whether the other kids cared or not. Seeing his pictures going up on the walls week after week acted on them, and we had a painting revival which swept up the most unlikely collection of artists. We had wanted the kids to write poetry too, as a way of breaking out of their blocks about writing 'proper' English. We had failed. A strange individual called Roy joined the group who was so clever and detached as to be completely unapproachable by the other kids. He wrote bizarre, surrealistic poetry — an endless stream of it — which was ignored by everyone for six months until he started reading it aloud in break times and writing word-game poems for the bottom reading group. There followed a wild poetry epidemic — poems during lunch-hours, maths lessons, on the backs of books, up the walls. Enough and good enough to fill a saleable volume.

These random flashes among the kids were the kind of proof we urgently needed that we were 'right about education'. But actually we still knew next to nothing about 'education'. All we were doing was blundering around, throwing in our ideas and occasionally, by accident, creating conditions in which the kids could educate themselves. Standing back a little from the chaos, we found some theory worth following. It had something to do with finding the right images at the right moment. Images from their own lives, 'relevant' images might be fatal as starting points. Talking about their flats, for instance, as the start to a lesson about cities, might only succeed in numbing their imaginations. They became depressed and mesmerised by the facts as they were. They didn't believe they could change the facts: there was no purpose in looking beyond them. Talking about the violence in Hornsey Rise might get the same result. But if we discussed Northern Ireland instead, which was 'nowhere' in their minds, and therefore couldn't worry them as an image, they might, by safe degrees, work back to the violence in their own lives which frightened them considerably.

It was a question of judging when the concern was there and near enough to the surface to attach itself to the right image. Having left home, Christine went through a stage of deep gloom about life and death which influenced the others in the group. It was the time of the Tutankhamen exhibition. In a typically irrelevant way, the kids enjoyed it immensely, and asked for lessons on Egypt. From burial rights we got to Christine and all her anxieties. Up to that point, she hadn't been able to talk to anyone about her fears. Had we organised a lesson on Death specifically to give Christine the chance to talk, she would, in all probability, have felt too directly pressured to respond. We could analyse easily enough what happened in such situations — in retrospect. The subject of the lesson had acted as a catalyst 'safe' enough to allow everyone to relax, close enough to a real source of interest in the group to act as a bridge to it. Manufacturing that situation in advance was another matter. We timetabled a lesson on 'dream homes' to give Sylve and Fran a chance to let out their bottled up furies about their actual home conditions. They saw it coming and retired behind a wall of giggles. We gave up. Two weeks later Mike and I were mending a door with our minds on chisels and screwdrivers. Mike began talking about his mother, what he would do if she ever died. Sylve and Fran were on the loose waiting for their cakes to cook. They wandered in to annoy us, failed, and started listening to Mike. The sight of Mike, the most defensive of kids, chatting so openly, trusting me not to laugh, acted as an invitation. They talked non-stop for an hour. I could cheerfully have strangled the pair of them.

It was so typical. We'd spent hours pondering on the best strategies for reaching them, designed clever lessons to do it, built up our energy to deliver them — and they'd laughed in our faces. They had to wait till I was tired, wanted a peaceful half-hour doing nothing but fix the Art Room door and couldn't have cared a damn about their love-hate relationships with their mums. Yes, they were learning, we were learning, but in all the 'wrong' places, at the 'wrong' times and according to nothing that looked like a system.

*

Right in the middle of this confusion of learning, our contract caught up with us. It was the autumn of 1971. Nine months had passed since the first five had come to us. It was time to 'attempt reintegration into normal school'.

7 The Centre of our lives

By the end of the first year we had become the founder members of our own exclusive religion. We lived and breathed the Centre all day every day and more of most nights than we now dare to remember. Ange and I crawled home each evening, and were still conducting our post-mortem on the day as we got into bed. When we met Pete at parties we would retire to a corner to continue our obsession. Our friends must have dreaded seeing us but were too sympathetic about our collective illness to say so. Our condition was very unhealthy, very necessary and very happy.

We had no choice but to carry the Centre round in our heads, because that's where it existed. The structure of the day and traditions of behaviour were still too fragile to drive on with their own momentum. Week by week we had to pour life into the place. If we lost impetus the kids became frightened and depressed, realising that their security rested on nothing more than ordinary people; the whole Centre collapsed into gloom. They had to believe that we were immovable and indestructible. The answer to the continual question 'Do you think the Centre will ever close?' had to be a rock-solid confident lie. We believed the lie too. The Centre was the only true place on earth. It was a brilliant, wonderful freak occurrence. The only way we could survive the pressure was by maintaining total solidarity with one another. Every Friday we arrived at the Centre together to plan the next week and congratulate one another on having managed to live through the last one. A 'proper professional relationship' was impossible and undesirable. We had to witness one another's ghastly mistakes at close range: misfired lessons that reduced us to haranguing the kids in the worst authority-under-threat manner, hitting out in panic when caught by unexpected crises, ducking confrontations we felt too weak to face. Our mistakes were never final; the kids would forget and forgive for the sake of their own security. But precisely because their own safety was so tenuous and therefore crucially important, the kids would attack our symptoms of weakness with deadly and merciless accuracy. My Oscar-winning brave fronts gave me no cover. A two-second pause in decision-making and A.J. would be into the gap with: 'You're chicken, and just don't know, do you? You tell us what to do and you don't know yourself.' If Pete, in depressed mood, showed a mere flash of rising temper in the face of Paul's endless wittering, it was enough to trigger reaction: Paul dancing around him, needling and whining: 'Go on then hit me, you great bully. Go on, just try. You think you're so big. Go on, go on.' So we had to watch over one another, ready for those moments, to come straight in with one hundred per cent support. We got the forgiveness because the kids could see that however weak we showed ourselves to be, they couldn't beat us. In all the times, singly and together, when we loathed our jobs, hated the kids, felt crushed by the trap of ultimate responsibility, we had that one thing to hold us. We couldn't take a day off, be late, sit back and freewheel, leave our load for 'the system' to carry awhile. We had ourselves and whatever we made was ours. None of us would sacrifice that for a more peaceful, less painful way of earning our livings.

Nothing beats seeing an idea becoming real. By September 1972 our idea had become eleven kids, a house adorned with murals, two classrooms lined with work, a daily routine of work, noise, learning and confusion, a collection of stray cases that felt like a group of people. If it was awful, then why did they come? Most of the kids came most of the time: an average attendance of over ninety per cent over our first three terms. They came because they wanted to be there, part of the group, part of the fun, of the action. And when they didn't want to be there, if the demands of the kids, the staff or their parents sent them running again, then they came because *we* wanted them there. A day missed and we were round to their homes, putting on the pressure. Our consciences were clear if it was the kids themselves applying that pressure: A.J. round pulling the charm on Mike, Fran after Sylve complaining she was lonely. But when it was us, 'them', the authority enforcing the law, there was need for a rationale. Put baldly, it was that we believed the Centre would make them happier, we thought that we could show them how, where and when they had already been happier there than they had been at home or on the streets. But in the last resort it was only us saying, 'Our idea works. You cannot deny that it does. We care about you and you're part of our idea. We're damned if we're going to lose you.' We couldn't begin to prove it with paper proof, certificates, or irrefutable facts. But, despite all our self-inflicted accusations of woolly romanticism, ego-tripping fantasy, we had flashes of strong certainty. There was the odd afternoon when the house was full of action: Chris and Tony painting quietly downstairs, Jane sewing a dress beside them, chatting to Pete, Sylve and Fran cooking upstairs with Ange, a group of boys with me building go-karts while teasing the girls. At the end of afternoons like that, sitting round the living room demolishing the results of the cooking, we could feel the relaxation spreading round the house — something real, happy and totally unprovable.

To say that we were introverted would be a gross understatement. Kids and staff, we were all absorbed in the life of our own enclave. It seemed, at that stage, had to seem, infinitely more real and vital than anything that happened in the outside world. Driving through London on our weekly visits out, A.J. acted as the Centre's comment-caller, the aim being to cause the maximum of embarrassment to the mugs in the street with the minimum risk of retaliation. Stopped at traffic lights in the City, we were being stared at by a group of bowler-hatted City-men: 'What d'you think you're looking at, you load of bloody penguins?' was the neatly timed remark as the lights went green. We were the in-crowd, everyone else a 'load of penguins'. The self-delusion was quite knowing. It was always the 'penguins' who had the power. The kids knew well enough that the dream would disappear, abruptly and probably without reason, like all else good in their lives. They merely wished to enjoy while it lasted that first-time sense of belonging somewhere as people, not just names and cases. That they deserved that sense, we were certain. What we couldn't claim, and had set out to prove, was that we were helping them to survive better in the 'normal world'. We could say, accurately, that we weren't providing a total 'escape' from it. The Centre opened at nine, closed at six and offered, deliberately, no refuge during holidays. Outside our hours of work, they had to face whatever their 'normal' or abnormal worlds had to offer. But there was nothing to show in our working time that we were guiding them towards coping with the 'outside world' they had all explicitly rejected — school. When we had space and time to respond to the pressures beyond the immediate, school came nowhere. Sitting on our doorstep there was quite enough to consider: Christine's brothers and sisters, locked out of home, hungry and bored; A.J., after rows with his parents, wanting shelter for the night; the local 'lads' with their plans for a youth club. We stretched to cover what we could see. When Chris, our first caretaker, a bus driver, left, we looked round for someone prepared to offer more than just guarding the building. By the time Sandy came to replace him the doorstep was getting crowded. It was the demands from within a hundred metres we were having to face. The demands of our schools, the pressure for 'reintegration' remained where they had been at the outset — on paper, in a theory we still felt bound to pursue.

8 Back to school — who's fooling whom?

We were heading for a very rude awakening. We can see it now, looking back; we could see it then but didn't dare admit it. It is painful enough to go over what happened, purely in terms of damaged pride. The thought of the damage we may have done to the kids by using them in our self-deception is hardly joyful either. But perhaps what galls me most of all is that, in admitting our failure, I must seem to be handing so much free ammunition to the 'enemy': a golden chance for the critics to say, 'Of course it failed. What did you expect? You treat them like babies in the womb, protect them from the hard truth about life, then kick them into the deep end and trust they'll stay afloat on nothing more than a warm memory.' I'll answer that one later. For now, I will just try to record what happened, with all the objectivity my extreme prejudice will allow.

The kids weren't the only ones who needed to see everyone else as 'penguins'. Our theory called for 'a close cooperative relationship with our two schools'. We had chosen, deliberately, to stay inside the existing state system. Running hard against this abstract rationale there was much that made us feel anything but cooperative. Our ambiguous welcome in the schools was followed by virtual silence. Only when making referrals to us were the schools obliged to break the silence, and, in several cases, beneath the background information given, there seemed to be a distinct note of challenge: 'OK, so we've failed to hold him. We believe he's a villain and a loser. But, if you insist, you may try to prove otherwise.' There were good reasons, beyond any accusations of paranoia on our part, for this apparent undertone. We were, by definition after all, out to prove that we could do something that the school had failed to do. By implication and in fact, we held different beliefs about the nature of education from those of our schools. Arguably, our strong introversion in the first year of life would have isolated us from the schools anyway, whatever their attitude to us. But the truth was, I think, something more involved.

Friday afternoons were the only times we had free to make contacts in the school. Through our first two terms Ange and Pete fought hard to resist the temptation of the more immediately rewarding jobs — talking to the kids and their parents, repairing the Centre — as more important than visiting our schools. Pete went to Archway, Ange to Tollington Park. Their experiences differed but the frustrations were the same. It was the year staff, the subject heads, grass roots level contact that Pete was after. But week after week, on entering the gates, he found himself steered off to see the Headmistress, or her deputy. At best he could only succeed in reaching a selected few, those favoured by the Head. Friendly chats, cups of tea and vague promises of cooperation 'in the future' were all he got. Before long he began to feel that he was merely being tolerated and contained.

Tollington Park offered more to Ange. In structure, it seemed more like a group of federated states than one school. A tight clique of long-serving Welsh Heads of Year as one state, the Art Department as another, Domestic Science, a cosy enclave by itself. She worked to build alliances where she could, and with some success. The Heads of Year formed a solid core of experience which held the loose elements of the school in a form of unity. They accepted Ange, shared their gossip with her and their real concern over kids in their charge. The Art and Domestic Science departments, laws unto themselves, offered chances of actual cooperation in joint projects with our kids.

With an enthusiastic probationary teacher in the Domestic Science department, we worked out our first joint venture. It seemed safe enough. She would bring a group of her sixth-form pupils to the Centre to meet Sylve and Fran. Together they would measure our windows for curtains and a few days later go out as a group to buy material which could be made up in the school by this joint team. The sixth-form girls came as planned. After an initial bout of chronic embarrassment, Sylve and Fran began talking to them, and ended the afternoon feeling friendly and enthusiastic. On the day of the outing, they became nervous again. During the morning Ange worked to calm them down, and by lunchtime they were ready to go. At that point we had a phone call from the Head of Department, who had returned from sick-leave, discovered the scheme and immediately stopped it. We were left with our two girls all keyed up with nowhere to go. The following day we received a letter of explanation. I quote it as a good example of the difficulties of cooperation — not in any sense as an attack on its author.

'When I first heard about the fact that Mrs W. had brought *our* girls along to Half-Way House I was just a little concerned about the feelings you might have. I know only too well from my pastoral care duties here over the last ten years as Head of House just how careful one must be over things of a confidential nature ... and when I heard the full story and the plans for the shopping expedition with your girls in tow, we got really rather concerned.

'B.W. is a Probationary Teacher and though full of enthusiasm, as you discovered, has not, I think, really thought the whole thing through — to include possible eventualities of such a jaunt. . . In any event — like all the things we do here — it is always the thing to get the OK from (a) The Head of Department (b) The Head or Deputy Head just in case the unexpected HORROR should occur. It does sometimes. . . I think . . . that it is absolutely super to have our girls make the curtains — but there is *no* need for them to come again . . .'

Angry as we were, we had to admit that we'd been excessively green, had ignored the protocol, forgotten the legal tangles of being *in loco parentis*. But inevitably our attitude hardened. The letter seemed like proof of our growing suspicions. We had learnt to accept the fact that fcr our schools, toiling over the problems of their fifteen hundred kids, we were of very marginal interest. Few of the staff knew of our existence or had the time to care about it. What we resented for ourselves and for our kids was the veiled assumption that the Centre's existence should be kept secret and confidential because its pupils were disturbed children who had failed in school. Worse than that, the letter hinted at a more widely-held prejudice: that truants carried some form of educational leprosy — a highly contagious disease — and should therefore be kept in isolation till cured. We began to wonder, though at that stage without evidence, whether the schools really wanted their truants returned at all. The teachers who knew and cared about individual kids at the Centre listened happily to reports of their progress. When we opened discussion about their return to school the smiles faded, the tone became pessimistic and anxious.

We persisted, reminding the kids that the end of their time with us was near, trying to discuss the mechanics of re-entry, encouraging them by pointing to friendly teachers they could rely on, the wide range of subjects open to them. The kids accepted their return as unavoidable fact. They were used to being the victims of decisions which seemed arbitrary and grossly unfair. When it had happened in the past, they had been able, at least, to vent their anger in hating 'the authorities'. But we had caught them in a vicious trap. They loved the Centre, dreaded school, didn't want to go back — and they trusted us. Yet it was us telling them to go back. We said we cared, they believed us, and there we were handing them over to the enemy, telling them it was for their own good, that we were doing it *because* we cared for their future. It was clearly understood that we desperately wanted them to achieve a successful return to school, even that the Centre's existence depended on it. The kids listened while we argued that they must grow tougher, more independent but that, of course, we weren't rejecting them — we would still support them. Intuitively they didn't believe us: they knew very well that we couldn't give them much support in school, we were as much outsiders as they were. Realising that they had to go back, all they could do was to try to deceive themselves into belief, hoping that, by some miracle, we would be right — they would be happy. Incredibly Fran and Paul actually volunteered to go first. It's a proof of loyalty from which, looking back, we can draw little comfort.

Back to school — lambs to slaughter

At first glance, Fran and Paul might have seemed the worst possible candidates for an early return to school. A.J., with all his social confidence, might have seemed a much better choice. But they were, however superficially, enthusiastic to try, and, however terrified of the outside world, they had, at least, got each other for support. Mr and Mrs Palmer were keen that Fran and Paul should start at Tollington Park School, instead of returning to Archway, together with their sister Lizzie who was leaving her primary school (from which she had been a chronic absentee). We all hoped that this arrangement might create a situation where, for once, the family Mafia might operate to support attendance. We tried to prepare the ground as carefully as we could. The whole family came to meet the Headmaster, Year teachers, class teachers. There was welcome all round, promises on both sides of support. It was agreed that we must all keep in close touch to avoid misunderstandings. The three Year teachers involved made it clear that they would watch over our trio. With a push from us Fran built up her role as Guardian of Attendance, threatening her brother and sister with instant death if they attempted to run out. Pete worked on Paul's enthusiasm for leaving. Together they planned out his timetable.

Their first day produced all-round tension. Having taken them in, we waited with other kids to see if they would stay. When they appeared at four-thirty, full of their achievement at having lasted the day, the kids remained sceptical: they knew all the routine lies. After expert interrogation they accepted the story and felt relieved. The relief held up for a fortnight. Then they were spotted creeping home during the lunchhour. The disintegration had begun. The walk-out had been over an incident of typically pathetic proportions. Paul had had a bad morning, had arrived in the wrong classroom, been thrown out, told off for wandering in the corridors and at lunchtime had gone with Lizzie in search of Fran; the three of them then attempted to go into lunch together, only to be told that they were in different years and must eat separately. The family unity had been threatened and they fled.

We fought to stop the retreat. The Year teachers told them to come to their rooms if they felt worried. We spent hours propping up their dissolving self-confidence. It was useless. After each fresh start, the incidents multiplied and they ran again. They were shouted at in corridors, asked who they were and where they had come from by teachers who didn't know them, became too frightened to go to their Year teachers, sneaked off without seeing them. The staff who had tried the hardest began to lose patience with them. Fran was blamed for leading them out, as a bad influence. The attitude grew less sympathetic. Our three became more axious and hopeless with every day that passed, retching or crying in the car as Ange gave them lifts to school. In a last effort to save the situation, Ange spent a whole day in school with Fran, moving with her from lesson to lesson. As the day went on, she felt increasingly pessimistic. Some teachers were struggling just for a semblance of order. By the time they had their class in their seats and had mustered sufficient pencils, paper and books to make a lesson theoretically possible, there was only just enough time for an attempt at teaching. The best of them managed somehow, through the barrage of gossip and interruptions, to reach the kids themselves, to discuss their individual problems, encourage and support them. But the maximum ration of attention to even the most vocal of the kids could never be more than three or four minutes in any lesson. Fran, sitting pale, tense and silent at the back of the class, didn't stand a chance.

Within three weeks their guilt and confusion seemed to have wiped out a whole year of our work. When they saw us coming to their flat, Fran and Paul ran in terror to hide over on the railway line with the other truants. If we went after them, they kept on running. Cornered, they treated us as they treated any other teachers, with silence, lies, anger and fear. The other kids watched the fiasco through all its stages and deep gloom settled over the Centre.

We had lost on all fronts. The parents could see all their suspicions about schools and 'those welfare people' confirmed. We had promised that the kids would be happy and had broken the promise. They blamed us as much as they blamed the school for mistreating their children. In the school the teachers felt disillusioned and betrayed. They had been told that these kids were 'better' and could cope with school. All their time and energy had been wasted. We had given the kids ridiculously high expectations of support and had left them totally vulnerable as a result to the most trivial of everyday irritations. For the kids in the Centre the sense of betrayal was worse still. We'd dragged them into a fantasy they had always known to be doomed. Having seen it destroyed, they were left with nothing but absolute certainty of their own forthcoming failure.

All our self-deception and double-think had surfaced to confront us. We had to spell out to ourselves what we already knew. The kids, none of them, were anywhere near tough enough, independent enough of us to have any chance of coping with school. As it was, we had created a situation of negative motivation for return to school. We were asking the kids to want to leave a situation where they were happy for one they hated. Having taught them to expect more from adults in terms of care and attention, we had made the impersonal atmosphere of ordinary school seem that much worse. We were, in unvarnished fact, teaching them to want what schools could never offer them. Even supposing we could succeed in getting them to the point where they needed less personal support and urgently wanted the range of teaching that the schools could, in theory, offer them, the jump was still too great. Our links with the schools were totally inadequate for the task: we knew too little, were trusted too little, had negligible capacity to support our kids once they entered the gates. I felt no less of an outsider than I had done eighteen months before, as a family caseworker. Our assumptions were under attack right down at foundation level. Working inside the Centre we had come to believe that what we were trying to create was not merely a specialised environment for a tiny aberrant minority of failures but an education which, as an ideal, all the kids needed and deserved. Suddenly, in this crisis, we were pulled sharply out of our 'alternative education' womb to face the view from the outside that our kids were seen as tiresome little misfits, and we as inefficient therapists.

There was no time to explore our confusion at leisure. The Centre kids were depressed. Fran, Paul and Lizzie were out on the streets. We had to act quickly to end the hiatus. We did the only and most obvious thing we could do.

'You mean, stay here for ever?'

With still no idea of what we *should* do, we felt certain only of what we *couldn't* do. We couldn't allow our three failures to remain out in the cold, paying the price for our misfired theory. Even knowing what it implied ('If you take them back every time how will they ever learn they must, one day, face up to the reality of the world outside?') we felt that we had to take them back. If we did that, then we couldn't carry on regardless as if nothing had gone wrong, pushing other kids over the edge. We were being watched very carefully all this time. Every day the kids probed our position, knowing that we were in deep trouble: 'You see, it's no good — like we said. Does it still mean I've got to go back? What'll they do to you now? 'Cos this wasn't suppose to happen was it?' There were growing demands that Fran and Paul should be taken back, that it wasn't fair they should be left out.

So we told them — just about everything we had thought about and decided. We couldn't have looked any sillier. By being honest we had little to lose and a great deal to gain. By the expressions on their faces, it was clear that they'd guessed our decisions anyway. We admitted that our gamble had failed, that the gap to be jumped in going back to school was too great, and that, in deciding not to send them back until we found ways of improving their chances, we were heading for a rough walk up the red carpet with the Education Authority. The morale graph made an instant leap upwards. Amidst the excitement and relief — 'You mean, stay here for ever?' — I doubt whether any of them heard or cared about the rest of our message: that we would still try to push them out to establish their independence, that we wouldn't be there for ever. They took only what they needed to know: they were reprieved.

We still had to brave the wrath and possible scorn of the Education Authority. We prepared our case carefully, stressing that we still wished to find a way of giving our kids the chance to enjoy what the schools could offer them. But our emphasis was changing. With fifteen months' experience inside us, we knew we actually had something to fight for. In spite of our failure to return kids to school (or perhaps because of it), we needed to insist that the Centre worked: the kids attended regularly, were learning, growing up as members of a group — much more than they would have gained walking the streets, more than they were prepared to do in any ordinary comprehensive. We weren't remotely satisfied with it. We were dangerously isolated, our teaching methods haphazard, we were devoid of viable exit routes for the kids who needed to grow out of the Centre. But there could be no fundamental retraction of our philosophy as it had evolved. There could be no withdrawal from closeness and honesty, the kids' rights to learn from involvement in the group, and the chance to practice their powers of self-determination. As we dissected the reasons for Paul and Fran's failure in school, we became convinced that their strength had been (if anywhere) in each other. We actively fostered interdependence — without Fran, Sylve felt cornered and alone, Mike was confident only when Jamie and Paul were with him. We had to ask that the schools should allow these natural groupings to remain intact in any attempted reintegration. More than that we needed a bridgehead, a base inside the school, somewhere secure and familiar from which the kids could move gradually outwards as they learnt to tolerate the structures of normal school. If they wanted their pupils back, our schools would have to meet us halfway.

We finished our statement and faced total embarrassed silence. It was ended by a mild round of 'we-told-you-so's'. Then we got our reply. Yes, what we had said might make good sense to us as a theory — but ... It just wasn't practical. The resources of our schools were already stretched to the limit. There was no space to give us the base we wanted within the schools. The timetable was already a computer programmer's nightmare; there was no way in which our friendship groups could be accommodated. How could these groups, drawn from different streams, of different ages, possibly be taught within the normal school structure? We were asking for more contact with school staff when teachers were already at breaking-point. As usual, we were seemingly naive. Only this time it had been a somewhat calculated move; we were trying to provoke an open admission. What both our Heads really wanted to say (and did say in later meetings) was that they didn't want their truants back: they had no time or facilities to cope with their needs. If they couldn't be sent back totally cured, they shouldn't be sent back at all. They were better off with us. With that fact on the table, we might have been able to start a 'real' discussion, as much about school failure as pupil failure.

There are, however, certain things you may not say as Head of a school — and that was one of them. Our Inspector needed a solution to the truancy problem, not an examination of fundamental problems in the education system. In the devious language of committees, the Heads were told to be cooperative — or else. With a semblance of evangelical fervour, it was agreed that we must all try harder. Attempts to return our pupils to school would be temporarily halted while we explored with the schools ways in which these children could be introduced more gradually to school life. There was discussion about creating some kind of stepping stone — a sanctuary inside Tollington Park School, for those returning, if only space and a suitable teacher could be found. The headmaster was keen but pessimistic. It didn't sound very convincing. Later non-events justified our scepticism. For the moment, however, we, like the kids, felt we'd won a reprieve.

9 Growing up — all down to us

The sense of relief evaporated rapidly enough. Only with its removal did we realise how much we had used the myth of rapid return to school as an excuse for not examining our own position fully. Since we had only half-believed the myth we had never tried seriously to organise the Centre's life around the demands of normal school. Nonetheless, on the pretext that we would only have the kids for a short time, we had semi-consciously dismissed as irrelevant the attempt to evolve our own goals for the kids. At minimum notice, we were forced to confront our Steering Committee to explain our 'position' and found ourselves (as so often happened) stating beliefs that we hadn't known we held. It took us some months, when the immediate crisis had passed, to absorb what we had said, trying to decide whether it was honestly what we believed. We decided it was.

We began to think about the kind of comments the kids had made at the time. Pete was telling Paul about the discussions he'd been having with teachers in Tollington Park; Mr. J. had said Paul could go to him whenever he felt worried, no one would be angry with him as long as he explained where he was going. Tollington hadn't been Paul's original school. Knowing nothing about it, he was struggling to believe the best. Tony, who knew the worst, was listening. 'Him, well he's a two-faced bastard for a start. All smiles and promises. But you just try it. You go to him and he gives you a right bollocking and sends you back to class. Really shows you up. Then the teachers won't let you go again.'

We were talking to Jimmy about the plans for his return to Archway: it had been agreed with his Year master that he'd be allowed to choose the options he wanted, riding in particular, as long as he came regularly. Jimmy and A.J. didn't believe a word of it. 'I've heard that before. If you ask for an option all you get is some rubbish about "let's just wait and see, we're not sure you're quite ready" — and that's it, the same every time. It just never fucking happens.' For all the kids, more or less, the view of school was the same: it used them, they could never use it; whatever was said, they had no power to choose; their opinions had no weight or value. If that was what they believed, then for them, at least, it was true. That

would be how school worked for them. It lay at the centre of their
fears about school, that they would simply be swallowed up by it
and forgotten.

What we had to do, then, was to teach them to use people and
their resources, which meant knowing what they wanted, believing
they were capable of getting it, and understanding how to get it. All
that was required was a total transformation. Looking at the Centre
as it was, we saw just how complete this had to be. It was the same
picture from all angles — in teaching, socialising, rule making and
breaking. The final responsibility was always laid on us, the teachers.

The kids believed it was their Centre — but only so far. When two
outside kids came in over a weekend and kicked a football through
the Art Room window, they were united in outrage: the criminals
should be brought in, worked over and be made to pay for the
glass — by us. When A.J. or Mike broke a window there were no
witnesses, no one had been there at the time, there were no
suggestions as to what should be done. A squatter borrowed our van
to move his belongings, and drove it into a basement area, leaving us
with a £200 repair bill and no van for two months. A simple lynching
party was the mildest of the remedies put forward by the kids. Forty
pounds of Centre money, money for their holiday, went walking and
all we got back was strict silence. Investigating their thefts, their
vandalism, stopping their fights, was our business. It was acceptable
procedure for us to shut them in the classroom, give them the
standard police interrogation one by one — 'Empty your pockets,
take off your shoes, explain your movements, admit you're a liar.'
That was the way the world worked: if the rules were broken, you
kept your mouth shut, lied where necessary, got treated as devious
scum as a matter of course. The only resentment against us was for
allowing it to happen. It was our fault for having the money to steal.
What made the kids angry was not following the procedure. If we
refused to play at being 'Kojaks', and insisted instead — 'This is your
problem, you know who did it, it's your money that's missing.
You've got fifteen minutes on your own as a group to find it' — then
we felt the outrage. We were copping out on our job, putting the
blame on them unfairly and, worst of all, asking them to break their
First Commandment — 'Thou shalt not grass on thy mates'. A.J.,
who had enough political skill to make sworn enemies believe that
they were lifelong friends, only once used that skill to solve a theft
crisis, and only then because he had a priority need to prove his
power to us.

This belief — that it was all down to us — held out against all
available evidence. Right in front of them, they could see that we
listened, changed our minds, carried out their suggestions. Seemingly

it made no difference. If they asked to visit London Airport and we went, it was still our responsibility that they got bored and didn't like it. There were moans about the timetable, requests for options — French, history, German, 'proper' school subjects. It was agreed that the system could only work if they stuck to their choice — the reasons were understood. Come Week Two of the scheme, that agreement didn't stop Fran, Sylve, Mike and his mates drifting off to join other groups and complaining that they didn't understand the lesson.

We were the reasons they wanted to change. I was the reason Sylve and Fran joined my history group. They didn't give a damn about the Spanish Armada. It just happened that I was their Hero of the Week, so they wanted to be in my group. Mike was in a 'Pete-phase'. Whatever he was teaching had to be good. Sylve and Fran were furious when I insisted on boring them. Mike blamed Pete for making him work. It was us that they trusted, not what we taught, not their interest in the subject, not their power to enjoy it. *We* had to have the answer, the power to interest them. It was our responsibility, our fault, our Centre.

Having fought to win their trust, we had to fight to lose it again in favour of them trusting themselves. We had failed to pull off the miracle of returning them to school. From there we had to go on to prove we were further fallible — but still useful.

Growing up — finding the proof

Success is often a matter of finding the right people at the right time. At the moment when we badly need fresh impetus, the right people arrived — Alex, Dougal and Richard. Richard came first, a longstanding friend, on a five-month student placement. When Sandy, our resident, left, a month later Alex, straight out of university with none of the theory and all the enthusiasm, arrived to replace her. Realising she couldn't live alone in the Centre, she invited in Dougal, a friend from university. Suddenly the kids had to cope with three new people, none of whom were wholly involved in day-time activities. Aware of the dangers of overstaffing, we arranged it that none of them would work full-time in the day. Alex had her evening duties, Dougal worked part-time elsewhere, Richard was only a temporary feature — and the kids knew it. But they had something to give that the kids badly needed, and to get it, they had to accept less than total involvement.

Richard had started teaching science with Sandy. Alex carried on where Sandy left off. It seemed from the start like the right direction. Conducting lessons round springs found on mountain sides was better than looking at rain-cycle diagrams in a classroom in London. But it was less than convincing simply because the kids hadn't started the spring themselves. It was just there, without visible reason. I had great success talking about the Origins of Life on Earth, plenty of attention and eagerness to learn from the kids. But when we went to the Natural History museum to look at the 'proof' of my unlikely story, I found Christine looking doubtfully at a dinosaur skeleton. She wasn't exactly saying it was a fake; she just couldn't believe it was real. Educational suppliers had no live dinosaurs for classroom use in their catalogues. But they did have chemicals which the kids could prove for themselves to be real and dangerous.

Simple science lessons became the most popular of the week. The sheer fact that they could make things happen fascinated the kids. They found that they could actually explain results using nothing more than common sense which they hadn't believed could have anything to do with 'education'. The fridge in the kitchen was full of bottles of ice in the process of cracking, crystals, sheep eyes, and rabbit brains. The rumour went round the butchers in the area that Alex was running a necrophiliacs' club. Science was a 'proper' subject and therefore safe: under cover of that image the kids began to accept what they had previously dreaded — being told that they could find the answer themselves. 'Proving it' became the current obsession. On a Thursday afternoon after the third call for Centre meeting, Mike and his madmen were still missing — an ominous sign. I blazed into the Art Room, ready to vent my fury. The three of them were crouched round a table, totally oblivious. They had swiped clay out of the Art cupboard, and using water as a lava substitute, constructed a beautiful working model of a volcano. They had proved a morning's lesson.

What was being proved was that doing things, making things wasn't necessarily an automatic flop, 'babies' games' or just a chance for a skive and a quick fag. In boring bloody maths ('What do I need it for? No one ever short-changes me') we got into traffic flow surveys, price comparison tables. The 'What-do-you-take-me-for, How-can-I-go-into-shops-asking-prices-they'll-think-I'm-a-right-idiot' routine was gradually replaced by 'Come on. It'll be a good laugh'. Even my terribly relevant, terribly boring Know-your-Rights lessons started to have some semblance of meaning. The morning after one of those lessons Rita came storming into the Centre, saying she was going to string me up. 'You and your bloody rights. Last night the Old Bill came round after my old man and I opened the door and says you can't come in without a search warrant and the bastard punched me right in the mouth.' It worked for me, not for them. But the other kids were impressed that she'd actually tried it. I changed my tactics, began again with teaching basic skills, like using the phone. By driving them to get their message across in twopence worth of time, daring them to phone large companies for information, I got them to discover that it could work for them. When kids in trouble came to the Centre, not for advice, but merely to ring up the Law Centre, I believed we were getting somewhere. They were learning to use people efficiently. Calls to the Fire Brigade tailed off as the kids discovered the phone to be positively useful.

There was nothing staggeringly original in any of this teaching method. It has all been preached and practised hopefully for years. But for the kids it was new. If their class had been involved in learning-by-participating lessons, they would probably have either been too alienated to join in or too frightened to be there at all. Or more likely still, they would have been in anarchic classes where the desperate teacher wouldn't trust his pupils enough even to turn his back, let alone send them on learning missions out of his sight. If it was new for the kids, it meant that it was something they hadn't already failed at. The chances of discovering success were higher. We had grasped that much, as a theory, early in the Centre's life. Practising it, however, we'd always had the uncomfortable feeling that most of our new activities were irrelevant gimmicks. What was the point, for instance, of giving the kids the chance to prove they could ride, or canoe? Gradually our scepticism faded. Paul, champion physical coward, proved to be an excellent rider. Fran, a non-swimmer, out-canoed A.J. with ease. Confidence carried over. When Dougal arrived it became even more apparent. He set up a darkroom and within a month all the kids could print their own pictures. The fascination of that magic kept the ever-restless Sylve shut away for two hours at a stretch. A.J. had always suppressed his artistic talents: nothing ever came out right, his pictures were torn up every two minutes. With Dougal, he designed and printed the Centre's own 'in-joke' T-shirt — a huge grinning cat and the words 'Super-Mong' ('We're not just ordinary Mongols — we're super-thick'). Everyone got them. A uniform at last. Other designs followed. If we'd been prepared for it, the Centre could have become a highly profitable T-shirt manufacturing company.

Machines could be an obvious short-cut to self-confidence, but usually the novelty value wore off rapidly. The tape-recorder was an exception. It was a mirror. It could prove to the kids that they existed. Sitting in the office recording crazy conversations to be played back and laughed at over and over again remained the most popular game year after year. The attraction of the 'reflection' was such that weak readers like Fran and Jamie who wouldn't write more than a dozen words to dictation before slumping back in despair, could sit in deep concentration for half-an-hour writing out their own tape conversations.

Perhaps the best example of self-confidence growing from a successful act of creation involved the use of the tape-recorder. In March 1973 our daughter, Leila, was born. A month later Ange returned to work plus baby. It was a direct threat to Sylve, Fran and Lizzie who had always clung to Ange as their all-providing mother-figure. All three felt painfully split: it was a dear sweet baby that deserved immediate strangulation. One day Fran would come in with a present of baby clothes, the next she was screaming for the bloody little animal to be taken out of her lesson. Sylve swamped Leila with love — and dangled her out of third floor windows to admire the view. One afternoon they demanded I should do a tape-play with them. Beginning with no ideas at all, they evolved a story about a baby who was kidnapped from its doting mother (Fran) by a lonely Irish girl (Sylve), and eventually got back, after multiple traumas, with the help of the police (me, naturally). The whole brilliant improvisation ran for twenty minutes, even including Leila's cries at the right moment on the sound-track — just in case anyone missed the point. Bursting with their own genius, they made everyone in the Centre sit down and listen. They had made it and it was good. It was also an open admission of their dreadful thoughts about Leila. Having turned their feelings into a drama, they began to accept that Ange was not their exclusive property.

Growing up — and out?

The sword of Damocles still hung over our heads: cooperate with your schools — or else. Even without the implied threat to our existence we wanted the cooperation to be more than a peace-keeping gesture. We couldn't, and deliberately didn't try to, provide the kids with a complete range of facilities for learning. If they weren't to become trapped in and crippled by the cosy world of the Centre, they would have to realise that there was learning worth having beyond our walls. We needed a range of possibilities which could spark motivation strong enough to carry them out, so strong that the price of having to submit to different rules and limits would seem worth paying.

In our schools, the initial burst of hospitality which followed the crisis meeting was depressingly short-lived. Very quickly it became obvious to both sides that they could in fact offer us very little: the Craft departments were at full stretch dealing with the extra demand created by the raising of the school leaving age, the sports facilities were fully booked. It was the same story in every department — except Art. Tollington Park's Head of Art made a heroic sacrifice — her one free period in the week — to give us the chance to bring all our kids in. It was the 'wrong' time — Tuesdays, late afternoon, the traditional time for outings. Even though the kids resented the change in their usual habits we decided we would try. Gathering up their courage, the kids marched in a tight group into the Art Department. They were happily surprised at the range of facilities and the afternoon seemed a success. It worked for two more weeks, and then we hit solid resistance. What was the point, they said, of being brave, risking being laughed at as outsiders by the kids in the school, for a subject they believed they could do at the Centre. The price wasn't worth paying. Suitably saddened, we had to give in. The loss wasn't, however, total. Tony kept going, week by week, working towards 'O' level. Some of the other kids began to wonder a little.

There is more to the world outside than just school. Every week, from the beginning, we had taken the kids on visits. There was always some restriction to be confronted: notices demanding quiet, enforced by shouting wardens, inevitable caretakers, old ladies to be shocked by swearing, instructors who required total obedience. We pursued a policy of no protection: if the kids infringed rules, angered wardens, irritated the public, then they would have to take the consequences — we would not cushion the impact. In the early months, when the kids were still at the exclusive Mafia stage, they constantly insisted that we should guarantee their sympathetic treatment. 'Why d'you let that little Hitler throw Sylve out? She was only joking. It's unfair.' 'That idiot just picked on Jamie 'cos he knew he was weak. It was obvious he was just looking at things. You're all fucking mouth and no action. You reckon it's unfair for kids to get picked on in the Centre but out here you're too chicken to say it.' We had to let them go on feeling betrayed until they realised that no one besides ourselves knew or cared a damn about the fact that Sylve couldn't help swearing or Jamie wandered round in a dream, picking up precious objects for inspection. Our power ended at the front door of the Centre. Beyond that line the people they met weren't obliged to be 'fair' to them. Gradually the message got through. Sylve was threatened with instant mutilation if she didn't keep her mouth shut, Fran kept close beside her as a walking muzzle. Kids who were ejected received progressively less sympathy — it was their tough luck.

In our second year we started roller-skating at Alexandra Palace every week. Out on the rink the kids became relaxed and happy, the most awkward, gangling kids were transformed: Sylve and Roy, total non-athletes 'on dry land' were our champion skaters. Having to mix with other school-kids using the rink was a price worth paying for the pleasure. One afternoon Kathy, a recent addition, an agressive, bright half-caste, became victim for a crowd of West Indian boys. Always sensitive to possible persecution, she retaliated immediately. In the wake of the fight we were threatened with exclusion if any further trouble occurred. The kids felt outraged and divided. No one disagreed that Kathy had been picked on. No one wanted an end to roller-skating. Kathy herself was outraged: what she wanted was revenge. During the week up to our next visit subtle group pressure was evidently at work. When we got onto the rink again Kathy found herself surrounded by a bodyguard of boys. For the whole hour the shield remained around her wherever she went. The expulsion never happened.

When the chance came for regular sailing lessons at a nearby base run by the Education Authority, Kathy was among those who volunteered. The instructor had been warned to expect 'special kids'. After he had made the discovery that, despite the warning, they looked like ordinary human beings, I suggested that it would be quite safe to treat them as such. Out on the reservoir he imposed rigid naval discipline, expected immediate obedience and no questions. Privately the kids thought he was hilariously funny but they wanted to sail. No one disobeyed his orders at any point — not even Kathy, who was usually the first to hit back against anything she saw as arbitrary authority.

By the time we found a video expert to run a film project with the Centre, most of the kids knew what to expect in working with outside specialists. It gave us another chance to try cooperating with our schools. The extra-mural studies department in Tollington Park suggested that five remedial stream pupils, at a loose end in their last year, should join in the project. The filming itself was a success. The result was a documentary with interviews and commentary on local housing problems. The intended cooperation was another matter. The kids from Tollington Park clearly looked on filming afternoons as a legitimate skive. When they turned up, which was less and less often, it was mainly to chat in the background. In their eyes, there were no restrictions and no obligations to join in. It was not what they expected education to be.

Harry came, a term or so later, on placement from a film course, to carry on the project. This time we had no offers from the schools. He was a quiet, gentle, passive character; our first thought was that the kids would demolish him within the first ten minutes. But he was the expert and that was what mattered to the kids. By the end of a summer term, they had made four films with him, including a twenties spoof robbery drama set on the railway line, and a view of our local primary school run over Kathy's commentary on her time spent there. A teacher from Archway School who visited the Centre every week and who, with her husband, was organising an end of term film show, suggested that we might like our films included in the programme. We suddenly felt wanted. A group from the Centre attended the first night, a feat in itself, and came back proudly claiming that our entries had been the best, but asking why no one had said the Centre had made them? The next day the Headmistress informed us that our films had been withdrawn for the rest of the week. We were not officially part of the programme and two of our kids had behaved indecently during the performance in front of the governors. We were depressed at how difficult communication seemed. The facts were that the teacher in charge of the shows had forgotten to tell his Headmistress about our entry and that Kathy's zip had broken when she sat down, and Sam had been trying to fix it. In retrospect apologies were made to us but the damage was done. There were times when we appeared doomed, by our isolation, to remain suspect outsiders.

Finding allies among school staffs of eighty or more was a slow and random business. It took us two years to find Jeanette, a remedial teacher in Tollington Park, who was willing to come in to teach once a week. The kids accepted her coming easily enough. She was proof that their school's teachers weren't all uncaring. By coming in to us, she triggered off a series of movements out. Jane was convinced that she must learn to read and Jeanette persuaded her to attend the Remedial Typing course she was running in the school. The motive was there. Jane went four times a week for a whole term to complete the course. The other girls began to envy her determination. One course wasn't enough for her, but it was all the school could offer at the time. So Jane enrolled at Sight and Sound and raised half the cost of the course herself. More than anything else, she dreamed of getting out of the depressed, debt-ridden life of her home and making a success of her life. Three more girls followed her lead and went through basic typing courses.

It wasn't 'return to normal school attendance'. But little by little the kids were realising that there was learning worth having at a price worth paying, outside the Centre.

Growing up — something like democracy?

'It's no good any more. It was better when we first started — just the five of us. We knew where we were then. Now it's one big mad bloody circus.' As veterans, Fran, Paul and Sylve, quite frequently, in gloomy moments, went in for little orgies of nostalgia. They were right enough to claim it was different. By the end of our second year we had sixteen kids. The original trio of staff had been added to and temporarily subtracted from. Ange had been temporarily replaced while she had Leila, resident workers had come and gone, there were part-time students and specialists to cope with. Kids could no longer expect individual attention as an immediate right. The Centre had become a busy moving human machine. They had to find their own place in it, or get left behind. We had started out as a benevolent fascist state but were shifting all the time towards something else.

I believe that we, the staff, started as we had to, as *the* authority. The Thursday afternoon meeting was included from the start as our idea of democratic forum, but it was a long time before it remotely resembled anything of the kind. The kids saw it as the staff's weekly moan-and-announcement session. Nothing in the Centre looked so much like a school class as that meeting. The kids shuffled, coughed and giggled in embarrassment throughout. All that business about asking their opinions was rubbish, a con, one of those educational games we played that they couldn't, and didn't want to, play. It wasn't how the Centre was run by us or by them. Our job was to make the rules, hand out the punishment, take responsibility for everything they did. Theirs was to operate as a second-tier clan — with us or against us. Ideally, clan rule allowed no dissenters — either everyone went on the visit or no one did, they all hated Pete and I or everybody liked us. When the single clan fragmented, the strongest of the cliques, A.J.'s lads, still ruled when it came to important decisions for the whole Centre. The nearest the meeting got to discussion from the floor were the brief skirmishes over power between rival factions. The stubborn individualists — Roy, Tony, Jane — had nothing to say. Yet there was one incident in the middle of this deadly stage of limited factional warfare that showed us how much better it could be, and how difficult the changes would prove.

Christine's loneliness had ended when her friend, Sue, joined the Centre. Much more mature than the rest of the girls, they exerted, as a team, considerable influence. In this instance it was over a perennial problem — nits. For most of the kids the nit problem had been a recurring source of public embarrassment all their lives, being shown up in class, getting the dreaded head torture from the Health Department's local 'Nitty Nora' every time she had visited their school. We had been able to do nothing about it. It was all very well for us nice posh teachers to go on about their going to the clinic; it wasn't us who suffered, we could afford to live in clean homes. But Chris and Sue wanted to be clean badly enough to go down to the clinic. It seemed to them grossly unfair that having dared to do it themselves they should have to face getting reinfested in the Centre. They explained the problem to the clinic and came in the next day armed with shampoo, combs and detailed instructions. Having cajoled and bullied the other girls into agreement, they came to us for support in forcing everyone in the Centre to have their hair treated. A.J. and the boys were furious: their power was challenged, they were going to be humiliated by the girls. But the logic was too obvious to avoid. Everyone, staff and kids, got done. The sight of a house full of shampooed heads was too funny for anyone to stay angry or embarrassed. No one could blame us — we hadn't organised it and moreover we too had nits. From then on, regular head inspection became an unquestioned routine. It was very clear, however, that the issue involved had been exceptional, something that affected everyone and about which there could be no real argument or opinion. Over anything else, consensus would have been almost impossible to achieve.

When a united voice did begin to appear in meetings, it was, perhaps inevitably, a conservative one. It was much easier for the kids to agree over what was already known and accepted. We wanted, for example, to change the term's holiday site. We'd been three times to the same place in Wales and were arguing that it was time for change. 'How do we know it'll be as good? It can't be. What's the point of changing something good?' We couldn't guarantee they would like it. Lunches, another issue, had originally been made each day by one staff member and one kid. With growing numbers, it was becoming impossible for two people to get the meal ready on time. By the end of second lessons the kids were complaining angrily about being hungry. But they didn't want the system changed: 'There's no room in the kitchen for more people. We don't like working in pairs.' Pretty evidently, too, they were getting bored with Tuesday afternoon outings. We suggested a change. The kids were angry; they felt it was a manoeuvre to deprive them of their weekly treat. 'But you're getting fed up with it.' 'No we're not. Take us to some new places.' 'It's up to you, as well as us, to suggest places.' Silence.

We were up against a familiar problem: what do you do if democracy doesn't produce the 'right' results? Over these three issues we operated a power of veto. In our superior wisdom, we believed that the kids had to be pushed through changes faster than they would have wished. Overriding their views, however justified, left a major problem unsolved: the kids could still legitimately complain about the results of our decisions.

At least they were beginning to push their views, even if they were largely negative. We didn't feel discouraged. Sooner or later they would make a decision and get caught out themselves by the consequences. The first decision to boomerang on them was a ban which they thought had been aimed only at us. The Centre had become a major attraction for educational sightseers, and nearly every day we had visitors at the door asking for guided tours. The kids felt, quite rightly, that the place was turning into a zoo for 'our lot'. They didn't want to be the exhibits. We agreed. The decision was taken that the Centre would not be open to visitors — ours or theirs — during school hours and we would restrict our visitors to Monday afternoons. In their enthusiasm at having won a victory over us, the kids forgot the ban cut both ways. A week or so later, one of A.J.'s mates wandered in at breaktime and we asked him to leave. When A.J. complained, we reminded him of the decision we had all taken. Revelling in the sight of our local genius getting clobbered by his own cleverness (it had been A.J. who had raised the issue in the first place) the other kids supported us. Exit one visitor. A.J. loathed being beaten. If he was going to lose, then so was everyone else. Thereafter he appointed himself guardian of the rule.

The question of lunches came up again. By now the kids were enjoying working in pairs and feeling self-confident. We were in the way, they said. They wanted to make lunch on their own. It was another smart move aimed at us. If we weren't watching over them, making lunch could be more of a laugh, a chance for fiddling the money while peeling the potatoes. The motion was passed. A month later, lunches were becoming late, expensive and bad. At last we had the chance to moan at them. They were responsible for the rotten food, not us. The kids admitted, readily enough, that the meals were bad but they resisted relinquishing their control. After a temporary revival, the standards dropped again. We needed some powerful incentive which didn't involve the staff. The kids suggested a weekly competition — with prizes, of course (the world doesn't run on pure pride in achievement). The new system worked. Lunch-voting each week developed all the characteristics of the fight for Presidential nomination; threats, blackmail, vote-buying with the offer to share prize-money — a real education in the unacceptable face of democracy.

They were learning. The first time we raised the matter of sanctions for lateness, the kids had been full of viciously punitive ideas: cold showers, getting thumped by A.J. (his suggestion, naturally), long runs, ten pence per minute overdue. Weeding out the impractical and the illegal, we arrived at extra work in break. Second time around there were protests from the regular late-comers — Mike, for instance, who had nearly five kilometres by bus to come every day. It was beginning to dawn on everyone that being fair was far from simple, particularly over such vexed issues as stealing.

Late in our second year we had a spate of thieving. The long inquisitions were exhausting and depressing for both sides. The uninvolved majority of the kids didn't see why they should suffer. That Fran, Sylve, and Lizzie were responsible was common knowledge. When we finally caught them, we were determined to stop them once and for all. For the next term, we said, they would have to take it in turns to look after the money. If it went walking, they were responsible. The deal was made in private but, as with everything else in the Centre, within twenty-four hours everyone knew. Nicking stopped. When our three would-be kleptomaniacs had served their term, we suggested the system should apply to everyone. Having trapped themselves into accepting responsibility before, the kids were highly suspicious. The idea worked. Only one person at a time had to carry the money — and the can if it disappeared. But by this stage in the game they could see further than that. If money *did* disappear it would be the unlucky carrier, rather than us, putting on the screws for its return, which would involve a breach of the First Commandment. It was a clear sign of the amazing distance we had travelled that, at the end of long arguments, the idea was accepted.

Learning to make decisions is a long and exasperating business. It took weeks and months of half-hour insult-shouting matches before the kids realised that they would actually have to listen to each other occasionally. Yet how different this was from the long silences of the year before. The loners got angry, demanded that we intervene and stop the time-wasting. It was very tempting to cut short all that meaningless, ear-splitting noise — except that it wasn't meaningless. By the end of the third year we could conduct something very like a reasonable discussion, discussion which even if it was still dominated by the main cliques (what else is a political party, anyway?) allowed the individualists to have their say. When a television programme was made about the Centre it was Rita, who, normally contemptuous of the petty wrangling of meetings, asked 'What protection have we got over this film? What's to stop them putting in stuff we don't like?' She was voted in as kids' representative and went with Alex and myself to vet six hours of film on a Saturday afternoon. Lizzie was the smallest, most socially ineffectual of all the kids. Throughout her first year, she did nothing but giggle and shout obscenities in meetings. But in the meeting, already referred to, when A.J. faced the whole group saying they supported our decision to take him to the police, Lizzie was the person who said it loudest and clearest.

Not only did decisions take longer to make, they took longer to implement too. Having decided they wanted to run their own end-of-term party, the kids argued for two weeks over where to hold it and who to invite, and nearly wrecked the party as a result. Given freedom to choose which group they wanted to join, when it had been decided that the Centre should split into three parties going to different places for the holiday, they chopped and changed their names on the list till the whole thing became illegible. But out of superficial chaos was emerging a working democracy: there was a party and a holiday and the range of the group's understanding was growing. Frequently, for example, we complained to each other that the kids assumed that Centre funds were endless, that money could always be magically found to pay for their damage. We never involved them in our discussions of finance — they didn't want to know. It wasn't until, as part of a maths lesson, Ange gave them a breakdown of holiday expenses, that we discovered that, by then, they did want to know. Discussing expenditure, allowing kids to run the office, we shifted nearer to it being *our* Centre, both sides included.

Anyone joining the Centre in its third year of life, kid, staff or student, had to learn about a very complicated animal. New kids learnt much faster than new adults, because it simply wasn't the teachers' show any longer. At first sight any random half-hour's worth of free time seemed just as noisy and anarchic as it would have looked in our first weeks of existence — perhaps even more so: kids in huddles on the stairs engaged in plotting the crime of the century, kids in odd corners chatting to staff, kids in the kitchen teasing, skirmishing and kids going 'nowhere' bounding back and forth between the various scenes. Learning to live in the Centre meant absorbing all the immediately invisible webs of rules and relationships that ran behind all that chaos. New kids had to learn the patterns: that Jamie, weak as he looked, couldn't be victimised, that A.J. was flash but no longer boss, that he would be protected as long as he joined with the group and didn't try to act clever, that if he broke windows he would have to replace them, that washing-up got done by rota, like it or not — on and on. They learnt in two weeks what new staff took six months to understand.

To add to the learning problems, no situation remained stationary for long. Jane might be talking to no one for a week because she was angry at having to leave the Centre. The next week, having got over her anger, she might be joining every group going in an attempt to get the most out of her remaining weeks. An inseparable pair one week, A.J. and Sam might become totally split for a month afterwards, both in pursuit of the same girl. But, for all its appearance of impermanence, the Centre grew stronger all the time, absorbing crises — such as Kathy trying to demolish the kitchen in a burst of fury that would have broken the group completely in our first terms. Pete Davis left, Pete Gurney came in his place, the original five began to leave, the timetable changed. The Centre went on growing.

10 You can't please all of the people, all of the time

Way back, we had dreamed that everyone was going to love and understand us — the schools, the parents, the neighbourhood. As it turned out, we frequently believed that we could please none of the people, none of the time. We hadn't set out to create an embattled enclave, a Summerhill-type paradise in enemy territory. But whomever it was that we were serving, it looked less and less like our schools. As the kids became more self-confident, and the Centre more democratic, it seemed increasingly unlikely that any of the kids would choose to return as full-time pupils. That they might, instead, learn to use the schools for particular learning resources wasn't exactly what had been demanded. While we continued our search for allies in our schools, we had to look elsewhere for support.

According to our philosophy, the local neighbourhood ought to have been our chief support: like so many of our original theories it proved to be ridiculously simplistic. We found ourselves living with not one community, but three, trapped in uneasy coexistence: the long-time residents of Cromartie Road, wearily outraged at the Council's destruction of their once-respectable neighbourhood; the depressed ex-homeless dumped on the large, decaying estates on either side of us, desperate for support of any kind; and opposite, the up-and-coming residents of the new estate, anxious to defend their hard-won status and contemptuous of those who had failed to 'help themselves'. Amazingly enough, considering the treatment they got at times from our kids, our next-door neighbours stood by us. When the kids asked them for a quote to put in our Third Year Report they remarked how much better behaved our pupils had become over the years. But across the road in the new estate we were regarded as an open cesspit for every evil in the area: every crime committed in North Islington was planned at the Centre, we were all drug-addicts engaged in orgies of sex and violence. For the old-age pensioners in the flats facing us, we were a good substitute for television. They sat on their terraces, noting every bizarre happening with horrified relish. Growing tired of the scrutiny, we issued an invitation to all our neighbours to come to an open day. Only one old couple from the flats appeared in trepidation on the doorstep and were astonished when the kids gave them tea and cakes. The rest stayed away. The fantasies were obviously much more fun than finding out the facts.

We hardly helped our reputation by welcoming all and sundry in the evenings, and mainly those from the old estates. Our basement Youth Club, having been started for Centre kids and close friends, grew to be the main (and only) attraction in the area. At its height, we had eighty kids per night through the doors, some from four or five kilometres away. Dougal, who bore the blame for the success, worked desperately to keep the peace. Offering the premises to the old people for bingo sessions effectively silenced their criticism for a time but the message from the flats remained unchanged: Yes, of course, the kids need a club, but not where we can see it and suffer from it.

At least we could claim that we were giving the kids something of what they wanted and needed. For them the Centre became that weird Free School place where the teachers were a bit soft-in-the-head but talked to you, gave you coffee and advice when you asked for it. At any one time Dougal and Alex would be carrying half a dozen major problems for the local kids as well as the work of the day-time Centre. We could easily have turned the Centre into a crash-pad, advice bureau, job agency, crèche — all the facilities the area hadn't got and urgently needed. We didn't, because we believed that, however limited it might be, our main job had to be helping the sixteen kids in the Centre. And real help for their kids was, of course, what the parents wanted. If their children were happy at the Centre then they should have been happy too. Except that the logic didn't work.

Giving help to the kids in their own right had been one of the prime purposes in the creation of the Centre. It was their needs we considered first, not those of their parents, which might be difficult and conflicting. If we were to act in the best interests of the kids as we saw them, we couldn't then hope for any easy role as neutral mediator, trusted friend to both sides. It was inevitable and even necessary that, for much of the time, parents should regard us with profoundly mixed feelings. What was surprising was not that they were suspicious of us but that they trusted us at all.

We had no typical parents. Frank and Flo Palmer, Fran, Paul and Lizzie's parents, were, above all, a law unto themselves. But their reactions to us were so extreme and contradictory that it seems worth describing them at length. Numerically, if for no other reason, they have the strongest claim to be quoted — three-sevenths of their family came to the Centre. For better or worse, they were with us from the start.

As a family, they were the world's Number One Victims. Their flat was number 13 — the Council renumbering it 21 didn't change anything. When their block was flooded, their flat was the worst hit. They had the nastiest neighbours, the most broken windows. In their version of life everyone hated them, the caretaker, the schools, the police, the Council. Pavements weren't for walking on, they were for falling over on, cars were objects to be hit by, buses were manned by malevolent black conductors and went deliberately to the wrong places, hammers weren't for knocking nails in, they were for carrying in your pocket in case of attack. If Frank and Flo let their kids out of the front door, they were certain to be attacked by gangs of six-foot West Indians, corrupted by their friends, turned into drug fiends by hippy youth workers, victimised by teachers at school. There was only one safe place — indoors. Going into their front room was like climbing into an overcrowded womb, with a TV instead of an umbilical cord as the life-support system. Every square centimetre of furniture was covered with children. All remarks made from parents to children carried the same basic message: when in doubt — don't.

The Centre looked, at first, to be everything they had always wanted as the right school for their kids: a warm, protective substitute family to hide inside; we wouldn't ever hit their kids, we wouldn't let anyone else do so. We were near enough to their flat for a constant watch to be kept, to allow them instantly to recall their young when global disaster threatened (about three times a week, on average). Frank talked about his own school days: 'The teachers never had time for you. There were always beatings-up going on. You got picked on and nobody cared. It's no good hitting kids for not learning. It's not their fault, it's the school's.' As a grown man, father of seven, he retained his horror of violence. 'The Centre's different. I reckon all schools should be like that. With all our lot, we could have a school of our own', which would have been their ideal, and our worst nightmare.

Naturally Paul got 'picked on'. It was bad enough that we didn't stop the other kids doing it, and muttered dangerous rubbish about 'self-reliance' and 'learning through experience' by way of excuse. What was much worse was the change in their kids. 'They're arriving home at all hours and giving us cheek and Paul always wants to be out with the boys.' They could see we were encouraging it, filling their heads with wild ideas by dragging them to dangerous places like Wales. The thought of open choice, loss of safe limits, was Frank's second greatest fear: 'It's just like a bloody holiday camp. I'm against hitting kids but it was no bad thing when they had corporal punishment in schools.' His greatest fear, and Flo's too, was the very obvious one: 'The fact is, that Centre's become the centre of their lives.' We were at war for ownership of their kids and it wasn't a war they could afford to lose.

Their chief weapon was the taking of hostages: one of the three kept home each week (usually on a rota, so as not to anger the victims), 'to look after the little ones'. Our own weapon was blunt and 'unfair', the nasty reminder that, however much they hated us, we were still more acceptable than the alternatives — court, removal from home. Usually, however, the battle was conducted at a more subtle level. If they felt that their kids were becoming too involved with the Centre, growing up away from them, they began to undermine their self-confidence at home. At the end of one week Fran would be happy, relaxed, full of plans for boyfriends, projects she was going to do with Alex, how much her reading had improved. At the beginning of the next she would enter the Centre scowling and confused: unable to read a single line, backing out of lessons. 'My Dad says you're a load of hippies. Mum says I've got to be in by five.' Paul, keyed up for the football match on Wednesday, would arrive on Tuesday with a dodgy knee which 'My dad says I've got to rest up'.

Often enough it seemed that it wasn't us caught in the middle between parents and child but the kids themselves, trapped between home life and Centre life, unable to commit themselves wholly to either. We couldn't avoid the accusation: what right had we to blunder into these families, removing the kids, imposing our own alien values and thereby adding to the conflict? However insulated the Palmer family world may have appeared to those outside, it *was* their working solution to the dangerous problem of living — as they saw it. To argue that keeping all their offspring at home would inevitably result in court action and some kind of family break-up was factually correct but it wouldn't suffice as a justification for our involvement. Ultimately there was only one statement we could make, simply that we believed that what we offered was likely enough to make the kids happier to justify the risk of merely compounding the miseries. It was a belief which looked pathetically incredible when all we could see was profound confusion in the kids.

For the Palmer kids the contradictions were impossible to ignore and we had no easy compromises to offer them. They bounced between home and Centre, testing one against the other. Fran would cross-question Ange. 'Mum says that fifteen is too young to be out with boyfriends. I've got to wait till I'm seventeen. Is that right?' Fran was desperate to prove herself to her friends. If the humiliation of being a little girl in white socks kept at home went on much longer, she would probably have been driven to make some dramatically disastrous gesture. To be honest, Ange had to disagree with

Fran's mum. Armed with that, Fran would return home to continue the battle. After further refusal, Ange would be called in as reinforcements. With Flo on one side looking for womanly support in controlling her wayward daughter and Fran on the other sitting silent and defiant, daring Ange to back up her demands there would be precious little room to manoeuvre. But, after twenty minutes of tense negotiation, Fran would be the one in the middle, in an agony of split loyalties: if Ange copped out, didn't say her piece, then she would feel betrayed; if she did, there would be argument and she would suffer later from her mum's sense of betrayal. All she would want was for the conversation to end, whatever the outcome, just to end. The same process repeated again and again edged Fran nearer to the kind of freedom we believed she needed. As Fran saw more clearly how her family worked, the confusion got worse. Arriving in the morning with Lizzie, she'd be asked where Paul was. 'I don't know. Just don't ask me. Go away.' With her older sister carrying the burden, Lizzie was more willing to break the taboos. 'Dad's kept Paul back 'cos he's out of work and says he wants Paul at home to look after the little ones.' Fran hated Lizzie with pure family venom for this crucial disloyalty. What we had to say was cold comfort: 'That's the way the world is — full of contradictions. Now it's us against your family but you'll get the same problems with your job, your boyfriends, your kids. You can't hope to solve it all. You just have to learn to be clever, keep your mouth shut sometimes, keep your different worlds separate. Play along while you go after what you really want for yourself.' A hard message to take when you're fifteen and don't know who you are. We felt amazed and respectful when it became obvious that they were not only listening to that message but managing to practise it too.

It would have taken a Third World War to split up the Palmer family. There was never any danger we would have that on our conscience. But for some of the other kids, leaving home seemed the only answer, and we couldn't deny that the Centre had brought them to the point of leaving. When all they had was 'bunking off,' hanging around at home, dodging the fights, it had never been worth imagining that life could be any different. Rita learned to survive her dad's drunken nights of home-breaking, wife-beating fury. She hated it, but couldn't leave it — someone had to look after Mum with her latest injury and be there to protect the younger ones. Dreams of running away were just to get her through the bad times. Jane lived much deeper in her dreams. Dreams of being rescued by a white knight from a happier world. In the Centre, it seemed suddenly that something better might be possible: it was somewhere they could be themselves, where adults actually listened to them, treated them as people, not problem number four in a problem family. Jane tried to leave home. She wanted to live with Ange and I. She insisted through one long awful weekend that she couldn't bear it any longer. She couldn't go back. Loathing ourselves every centimetre of the way we made her do it. Rita hovered on the brink. It was always 'if' and 'when'. Her graphic accounts of each new horror were her escapes; an everlasting excuse for all the things she promised to do and never did. We told her that she couldn't spend the rest of her life blaming her failures on her family. Later no one would listen or care; she would merely be trodden on for her hopelessness.

A.J. not only talked about leaving home, he did it, on average, about once every three months. He ran to the Centre and stayed while we tried to arrange a compromise with his parents. When he couldn't accept the compromise, and we turned him out, he camped on front room floors, in derelict cars, anything rather than sacrifice his pride. Arriving at the Centre each day progressively dirtier and more exhausted, he served as a walking proof of what we had to say to the kids who wanted out. 'Yes, we believe that it's dreadful at home for you. But the facts are that you are fifteen, penniless, dependent, haven't got jobs, won't find anywhere to live, stand little chance of, and wouldn't want, reception into Care. Right now you are powerless. You must survive as best you can, toughen yourself up and plan for your freedom.' It was the last thing any of them wanted to hear: they needed final answers, drama and excitement, the heroic escape into paradise.

We must frequently have appeared to the kids as a group of hypocrites and fence-sitters. We encouraged Mike to be independent of his mum but when he went off for the evening without telling her, we agreed with her moans about him being inconsiderate. Sue was lectured about not trying to live her mother's life for her yet we supported her mum's complaint of how little housework Sue did. We helped Sam break away from his neurotic and alcoholic mother. When he discussed her problems with us, showing how clearly he understood how and why she had wrecked her life, we felt obliged to add to the pain of his insights by insisting he should try to support her a little. When Christine came to the Centre we encouraged her to grow down, catch up on the childhood she missed. When she left home and came to live in the Centre, we pressured her to grow up, get a job, visit her family regularly. It wasn't so much a fence we were sitting on as one end of a see-saw. If the Centre became too much of their lives, home life hit back: angry parents, guilty feelings, days kept indoors to even up the score. Pulled back inside the family, the kids took up their old roles — helping Mum, slumped in front of the telly, kicking bottles round the back yard. We had to begin again to lead them out, to rebuild their confidence, asking them to accept what millions of people twice their age couldn't accept, that their parents were only other people whom they hated and blamed and couldn't stop caring about.

The point of balance could never be known. Interfering with family lives was a bad enough strain on the conscience and the nerves. Realising we were playing guessing games with our interference was one stage worse. There was no textbook rule that made it unquestionably fair to let Christine leave her family without mothering of any kind, or Sam's mum without a prop, but to force Jane to carry her unhappy parents. The only certainties we gathered on the way to keep us going with our gambles were that the kids were at times stronger than anyone ever knew, survived the crises, coped with both worlds, and that their parents didn't hate us for what we did.

They had every right to hate us, and not just out of jealousy for taking their kids away from them. What we practised and preached was frequently totally opposed to their views on proper child-rearing. We let the kids swear when we should have taught them respect for their elders with a clip round the ear. We gave them choice when we should have made them learn what was good for them. Frank Palmer was not alone in thinking that the Centre was 'a bloody holiday camp'. But they cared that their children should be happy and fought hard to make it possible. Jimmy's mother was described in the file as 'indulgent, weak-willed and uncooperative'. She backed us all the way: supported us when we laid down a tough line, kept Jimmy in to allow us to collect him. Finally when we turned him out of the Centre, she accepted that as fair. She believed we had tried our hardest for him. Mike's mother had to watch her son growing away from her, but when his younger brother was offered a place at another similar centre she was genuinely pleased. Sweeping confidently into the parents' introductory meeting, she proceeded to tell all present how happy their children would be, how good it was for them to get away from home for school trips.

Certainly many of the parents often felt the Centre was unfair to them: they had a right to help too but we gave it only to their kids. There could be times when that wasn't true. Ten years of being told their children were disruptive, bad influences, problems, had done little to comfort the parents, they became too depressed to insist that their children were good enough at home, obedient and quiet. Apathy or guilty agreement were the only options open to them. We complained too, but the fact that we had accepted their kids as they were and had gone on caring gave us some right to an honest moan. Half-an-hour with Jimmy's mum, telling her what a little swine her

son was in hideous detail, was, perversely, the kind of support she
needed. It was assurance that she wasn't just a feeble mother: Jimmy
really was a pain-in-the-neck, she could relax the pretence and admit
it to someone who knew it too but hadn't yet given him up for lost.

During periods of cease-fire, Frank and Flo would be full of offers
of help for the Centre: gifts and stolen goods at bargain prices, new
kitchen units to be fitted by Frank in his spare time, their support
for a parents' association. 'Pity we're too old. We wouldn't mind
coming to the Centre ourselves.' It was more theory that couldn't be
practised: involve the parents, then they won't feel jealous and their
kids won't feel divided loyalties. At different points, the possibility
of having someone's mum as our cleaner was raised, only to be
vetoed every time by the kids, even though it meant they had to do
the cleaning themselves. It was their place, a refuge away from home.
To have parents around would allow the pressures to invade their
only private space. After three years of kids-only parties, it was
agreed to invite parents to our Christmas celebrations. Most of the
kids seriously wanted their parents to see their school, to show it off
to them, but most of them couldn't actually make the step of
inviting them. 'She'd show me up.' 'My dad wouldn't understand it.
He'd just say it was tatty.' As a compromise it was decided to have
parents and kids in separate rooms for the party. In the event the
half-dozen parents who came mixed happily with the kids, said they
were proud of them, bought drinks for them. No one got shown up.
We all danced and got drunk together.

Sitting around afterwards in the party debris, we relaxed in the
dream of how good the Centre could be. Parents proud of their kids,
kids proud of themselves, and end of warfare, of working in the
crossfire trying to explain the parents to the kids, the kids to the
parents. Even allowing for the high alcoholic content, we could see
that it was a possibility worth fighting for.

11 'There's no success like failure, and failure's no success at all'

'Of course, you do realise, don't you, that they won't ever want to leave?' That was the usual final comment, often accompanied by a triumphant grin, of our 'sympathetic' visitors. We had to put up with the accusation for three years without having any reply to make. At last we were about to find out the answer: Tony, Jane, Rita and A.J. were about to leave — or not. We had always faked complete confidence when faced with the question. Privately we were scared both ways: scared they wouldn't be able to leave, which would leave us wide open as having created crippling dependency; scared they *would* leave without a single proverbial backward glance, and confirm our fear that the Centre, we, had hardly touched their lives at all. If it was true that experience of the Centre had made the kids even less likely to accept normal school than they would have been otherwise, it was a dreadful possibility that we might have had the same impact on their job expectations, that they would leave in search of cosy little firms where they would have choice in their work and a voice in the management. We comforted ourselves against that thought by claiming to one another that all they wanted was money to buy their independence from home, from crawling to Dad on a Friday night, cash to act flash with their mates in the pub on Saturday evening.

The Careers master at Tollington Park sent us a set of pamphlets covering the multitude of possible careers open to school leavers. We sat down with our leavers and began to go through them: 'What do you need to be a nurse? Answer: a bright personality, at least five 'O'-levels . . .' 'A career in computer-programming. If *you* have an A-level in . . .' — and so on. Weeding down through the pile, we were left with a career in shelf-filling, how to become a meat-packer, what it takes to be a shop-assistant and a few more of the same. No one in the room was wide-eyed with enthusiasm. Of course the kids knew it all, anyway. So did we. Without qualifications, they and thousands of other leavers, were all bound for the dull, dead-end, cheap end of the labour market. It would have been childish to complain: it was of no interest whatever to anyone but ourselves that they were four real people with dreams and potential. What mattered was whether they could fill shelves, pack meat and pick up £16 at the end of each week. But there was nothing to stop us being depressed about it. We thought of how little we had given them. They might be leaving us as much more secure social beings, likeable people; leaving us, however, without trades, without qualifications of any sort. This wasn't, in fact, our first taste of the reality of leaving. Christine had been the first. She had been an artist, she had wanted to design clothes, and the Careers Office had found her a job in a dress factory where she laboured all day over a sewing machine, came home every night with chronic back-ache. If she had seriously wanted to be a dress-designer, Christine could have gone to Art School, which would have meant another three years of poverty on top of the fifteen she'd already been through. Tony could have made it too: he could easily have got O-levels, A-levels and have gone to university where he would have been able to carry on reading James Joyce in peace and quiet. Though he was loath to admit it, A.J. had the same talents as his father, a stonemason/restorer in the British Museum. With more patience, and a willingness to accept minimum apprentice wages for several years, he could have been a craftsman.

As it was, Tony had his dad behind him, bullying him every night to forget all his artistic nonsense and join him on the building-site. He needed money too — to buy records, to go to concerts, to be one of the lads. Rita didn't care, anything for a laugh, as long as she wasn't treated like a servant, taken for a mug and shown up, which she knew very well she was very likely to be. Jane had her typing and the dream of being a smart secretary in the West End. But literacy had come too late. For all her charm and bravery she still couldn't spell or read well enough to survive in an office. And A.J., he couldn't bear to think about it at all. It was too humiliating for the King of Hornsey Rise who so much needed respect. He wanted instant money — lots of it. His master-plan for a guaranteed £400 a week tax-free was predictably simple: 'Three hours' work, knock off two decent motors, and there you are. Dead easy, no trouble'. Except for the fact that, as a criminal, he was third rate, cannon-fodder for the courts, and would never get the chance to perfect his skills.

In their few remaining months with us, we tried to equip them with as much of a survival kit as possible: talks from Social Security officials on the art of claiming your rights, lessons on how to fill in forms correctly (the best response I got from A.J. was when I pointed out what a fool he'd look, asking strangers to fill in his forms for him), trying to drill them in the business of interviews. They gained something from it, but, more than anything they began to bury their inappropriate hopes deeper inside their heads, a painful necessity we took no delight in witnessing. We felt trapped by an unanswerable question: how did we make them believe they could and should fight for the best possible situation without encouraging them to become unemployable, frustrated drifters? Life wasn't clearly labelled with signs that read 'Stand up and fight' or 'Sit down and shut up. This one you can't change'. Whatever other changes we were prepared to accept as fair, we were determined that no one should be able to accuse us of having made our kids indoctrinated victims of our middle-class politics.

We needn't have worried so much: they weren't our kids or anybody else's. The Centre had just been one lucky thing that had happened to them. Luck came or it didn't. There was nothing they could do about it either way. They had learnt to trust a little more, to push their chances in life harder. They knew where to go for help if they needed it. All four were sad about leaving in their own ways. But they left. At the start of the next term they weren't hanging around the front door begging to be let in: Tony was working as an apprentice carpenter, A.J. was tiling roofs, Rita was on the line in a gin factory (getting her laughs) and Jane, having lasted a week in an office, was working as a child-minder in Highgate. They dropped in to see us regularly in the Centre and at home, but not to thank us for turning them into model happy citizens. None of them was model or altogether happy. Tony got fed up with earning half what his mates were getting for doing the same job, Rita's family went on fighting and drinking, A.J. was still a third-rate criminal despite his regular wage-packet. They were all surviving and still trying to do more than just survive. Survival in a vicious depressing city world is no mean feat.

Now, finally, I have to admit a problem of tenses. Neither the Centre nor its kids are dead. All are alive and living in Islington. I cannot, thank God, deliver any final epitaphs on success and failure. All I can do is to examine the omens, misleading as they may be.

We'll let you know in fifteen years

Nothing hurts as much as the first failure. Throwing Jimmy out of the Centre seemed, at the time, the beginning of the end; proof that we would never be able to help any of the kids. We learnt from him not to be so vulnerable and arrogant. What he learnt from us is open to question.

Jimmy grew up as a pawn in his parents' malevolent marital game, constantly used by one against the other. Living with his mother he was endlessly indulged, filled with stories of his father's cruelty. Out on the lorries with his father, he was told that his mother was soft and devious, and he was given lavish presents for listening. With manipulation as a way of life, Jimmy became an expert in the cynical art of using his parents in return. When he had pushed his mother to the limit, spent all her housekeeping money and humiliated her with every kind of emotional blackmail, he would disappear to his dad, claiming he had been thrown out. Within a fortnight his father would discover his wallet going short and Jimmy would be beaten for his cleverness. By which time his mum would have recovered her dignity, be ready to take him back — to begin the cycle again. There were no limits, no final reassurances of love. At fourteen, Jimmy was a beautiful, charming, miserable little boy, frightened of his own power, desperate for care without strings, convinced that no one would ever love him enough.

Never, in his year at the Centre, did he once stop playing his game. He didn't know how. He either had to be leader of the pack with all the kids firmly under his influence, or the lone, despised outsider. With the staff he was the archangel Gabriel or the Devil himself: eager, cooperative, answering all the questions, volunteering for the nastiest jobs — or disrupting, subverting, leading rebellions on the slightest pretext. Nothing was ever quite good enough. If he was taught in a group, he wanted individual tuition. Given it, he complained he was lonely. When we ate together, he wanted a table to himself. Offered two cakes after cookery, he pinched a third. He could never believe that rules might be unbendable. There had to be some way to bribe, bully or insinuate his way round them. Every time he found out that he couldn't, the scene was the same. Having given us ample excuse for committing murder, he would take the slightest touch on the arm as the cue for a 'dive' that made professional footballers faking a fall in the penalty area look like amateur tumblers, hitting every piece of furniture in the room on his way down (and tearing his new jacket into the bargain). He would storm out of the Centre promising to throw himself under the first bus he saw. The next day he crawled in overcome with abject contrition, and off we went again.

By the end of his second term, it was obvious that his game hadn't worked. A.J. had beaten him in the leadership stakes and he couldn't tolerate being just one member of the group. The other kids forgave him for his verbal torture and betrayal for as long as they could, and far longer than we ever expected. But inevitably demands for his removal from lessons grew — Jimmy became the first victim of the group solidarity he had helped to create. Returning to school seemed to him another chance to prove himself a beloved hero (because there had always been another chance). He asked for a change of schools and didn't get it (Tollington Park, his first choice, said 'not with a barge-pole'). Back in Archway he lasted ten days. It was too big a stage for his act to be effective. His options had run out. He couldn't accept school and he had exhausted goodwill in the Centre. We tried every tactic we could think of to draw him back but he came less and less often. Faced with an ultimatum, he didn't, for once, threaten dramatic suicide. He just drifted away. The kids worried about him, tried to persuade him to come back and us to take him back. He had a year of school left to run and nowhere he could go. At the time we were quite certain he would be under lock and key within a month.

With Sue, there was less soul-searching but much the same story. When her best friend, Christine, left the Centre, she couldn't make any new friends. In her case, childhood had been spent bouncing between one grandmother, several fathers and a mother who treated her more as a sister than a daughter. In the Centre she flirted with the boys, teased them into molesting her, then screamed for help. She asked to be treated strictly, made to work hard, but withdrew when we obliged. Under pressure, she could always retreat into being the supportive sister to her mum. When they moved out to Totten-ham, our fight to stop the collusion became hopeless — they were out of easy visiting range. Her attendance fell below fifty per cent. We couldn't allow a place at the Centre to be so under-used, so she was out.

Losing Roy, our poetic genius, was a much sadder affair. Super-sensitive, super-bright, he was the odd one out in a large family torn apart by bitter rows and aggressive delinquency. His brothers and sisters regarded him as weird, his father told him he was mad and destroyed all his incomprehensible creations. He couldn't afford to be hurt any more; getting close to anyone meant that his madness would be discovered. The Centre was the first place he had found where he was accepted as himself. We liked his poetry, Alex and Dougal wrote 'mad' comedies with him in the evenings. We tried to make him believe he was no madder than the rest of us. Though he never joined in the group, but kept himself as an amused and detached observer, teasing and enigmatic, he still achieved a status of sorts with the other kids. Roy was the Centre's court jester, re-spected for his brilliant eccentricity. For a year and a half he hovered on the brink of risking honesty, hinting at how much he hated his father, then dancing away, mocking us all. When we reached the point of breakthrough, he announced that he wasn't going to come any more. And he didn't.

The diagnosis for our failures seems quite straightforward: kids who couldn't become part of the group lost out on much of the benefit and incentive of belonging to the Centre. They couldn't learn from their social mistakes, couldn't see their image as reflected by the other kids or adjust their behaviour to meet what they saw. That we cared wasn't sufficient; we were, after all, paid to care. What kept other kids coming, through the worst of confrontations, was, finally, that they had mates who needed them there.

It's a good theory, very neat and true. The trouble is that, now, we can't be so sure that 'failure' is the right word to use. When we took Jimmy, Archway school told us he was a hopeless case, beyond all help, an evil influence. We interpreted their remarks wisely (it's amazing how clever we were on our first day) as a symptom of their anger at having been rejected by Jimmy: if *we* can't help them, then no one else can. Casting him out ourselves from our Garden of Eden, we knew that he couldn't survive without us. He did, damn him. He hasn't, as far as we know, been in trouble with the law since he left us (that is, he hasn't been caught). The latest word on the grapevine is that he's doing well in the Army, drives a flash car and is engaged to be married.

We can play that news in any of several ways. It could be that kicking him out was the best thing we ever did for him, that the shock of hitting a real limit for once in his life worked a miracle 'cure'. Or we could argue that we kept him off the streets and out of the hands of the police for just long enough for him to do his own growing up. Perhaps behind the successful front, he's still miserable and has just been lucky not to have had to pay a legal price for his misery. I can't quite accept any of those versions but, whatever the truth may be, we can't write him down simply as a 'failure'.

No more can we over Sue, even though she's still playing around on the edge of disaster. When last heard of she was joyriding in stolen cars, talking about jobs and never quite getting them. If she reaches twenty without experiencing unmarried motherhood, we'll be very surprised. But we have an 'if only' factor to save our face: if only she hadn't moved away we might have helped her more.

For a year after walking out of the Centre Roy stayed shut in his room. Then his worst nightmare was confirmed: he was locked up as 'mad' — placed, in fact, on a court order, in an adolescent psychiatric unit. He 'phoned us recently. His first words were 'You see, I was right. I *am* mad.' Later in the conversation he talked about why he had left the Centre: 'It was just to spite my dad. He found out I was happy there, so I left.' He may have been happy but the fact remains that we knew we couldn't give him the intensity of attention he needed to stop him committing that kind of spiritual suicide. I think we knew it, even then. But caring as much as we did about him, we couldn't admit that the Centre was the wrong place for Roy to be. It was our failure — not his.

But it would be a very masochistic form of dishonesty to take all blame for things that go wrong for the kids, just as much as it would be tempting dishonesty to take all the credit for their success. The Centre neither is, nor was intended to be an isolation unit, free from dangerous outside germs. We set up to help the kids where they happened to be. We have to take our place with all the other possible influences in their lives. If parents split up, we get unhappy kids, and have to start rebuilding security it may have taken years to achieve. If stealing cars, or sniffing glue becomes the latest craze in the area, we have kids in trouble and kids in states of pathetic stupor. If the kids somehow manage, in spite of everything their families, their neighbourhood, or we do to them, then we jump happily on the bandwagon.

Nothing I've confessed is going to stop me pointing to some of our dramatic success stories, even if I can't altogether explain them or prove what degree of credit we should take for them. In one sense we should take none of the credit. The kids whose lives have changed most for the better are those who learnt to use the Centre best. They saw what they wanted from us, took it and left, confident that they could find help elsewhere in the future when they needed it. Jane, spoilt, fragile and indolent, became the toughest person in the Centre; in two years she missed just two days of school. She used us as a platform for the determination she always possessed but had lacked a base for. She's still using us. For eighteen months she worked for Ange and I looking after Leila, and doing it very well. She left us six months ago and moved away from home, remaining a close friend. Mike used me as a substitute father when he needed one. With the self-confidence he gained, he was able, for the first time in his life, to find friends around his home. Just before he left the Centre he was charged with his new-found friends with a string of car thefts. Stealing cars may have made him a temporary social menace but, at another level, it was a fair sign of his success in becoming just 'one of the lads', rather than a neurotic teenager who went round wrecking the flats of his mother's best friends (which is what was on his record sheet before he came to the Centre). Whether or not the magistrates believed my 'typical social worker's excuse' for his delinquency, I don't know, but he was spared Approved School, and hasn't sinned since. He currently works as a messenger in the West End, earning twice as much as other kids who wouldn't have the nerve to venture so far from home to work. When he comes round for a drink to show us what a smart young man he's become, I feel entitled to my quota of pride in him, and allow myself to forget what a tough ambitious mother he has always had to drive him on.

Talking about Jane and Mike, however satisfying it may be, is a misleading luxury. The issue of success and failure doesn't, typically, possess that kind of clarity. That kind of transformation is more apparent than real. For most of the kids change comes so slowly that it passes unnoticed for much of the time. There are few decisive moments. Experience accumulates, leads to small adjustments, mistakes are made, learnt from, made again. Frequently the cycle seems stationary. Although we now believe we can spot with a developed instinct the kids who will benefit most from the Centre, we are still caught looking the wrong way. We were sure, for instance, that Janet would quickly prove to be an ideal referral: shy, insecure, academically bright, her parents profoundly unhappy with each other but determined to help us with their daughter. Yet Janet ran on her first day and kept on running. For nearly two years she stayed stubbornly on the fringes of the group, playing her role as feeble little girl for all it was worth. She would sit demure and silent during breaks, attracting the boys, being a focus for trouble yet never being responsible for it. Every time there was a serious chance of her becoming involved in the life of the Centre, she disappeared for a fortnight of mysterious illness. On at least five occasions we discussed throwing her out: she would take nothing from us, gave nothing to us. She was a passive, time-wasting parasite. When her father died suddenly, we thought it would be the final blow to our hopes of helping her. Her father had been closest to her, unhealthily close, the source of her imbivalence towards men. His death, we believed, would freeze her chances of ever resolving her deep mixed feelings. There would be nothing to stop her being drawn into cosy collusion with her mother. We carried on with our routine — collecting her, pushing her towards the group, confronting her with her laziness — out of force of habit. Our attention was elsewhere, and we hardly noticed her moving. Nearly three years from when we took her, Janet, the ideal Centre pupil, seems to have finally made it. The simpering voice has gone, she is right there among the strongest of the kids, arguing in meetings, coming on every Centre holiday. She has just taken English O-level.

With her in the exam hall was Kathy, whom we took, somewhat reluctantly, with every reason for expecting violence and an early ejection. En route to our door, Kathy had fought, screamed and smashed her way through one primary school, two comprehensives and two boarding schools for the maladjusted. We, and she, feared very much that the Centre would be just one more depressing trophy. Sure enough our crockery replacement bill increased dramatically. Her well-founded nightmare that everyone hated her drove Kathy to arrange one violent confrontation after another. But, unlike Janet, what she needed was obvious (to put it mildly). She knew, we knew. The Centre was her last chance to prove that she could be cared for and she would fight to make it work. So she has kept going through all the outbursts, the rationalising red herrings (telling us in lucid detail why she was 'maladjusted', how she had suffered through being able always to intimidate her mother — analysing as a substitute for changing herself). She will admit now that she cannot spend the rest of her life blaming her behaviour on her upbringing. She will clear up the classrooms she has wrecked, let us force her to repair the windows she breaks. Having seen her enraged, threatening Pete with a bottle, it seems incredible. But the fact is that, like Jane or Mike, Kathy has a rock-solid determination to succeed. She knows how to use us.

The one kid whom Kathy cannot intimidate, who says what she likes to her and won't back down, is Lizzie, the baby of the Palmer trio, the smallest person in the Centre. We have always seen the Palmers as our long-term burden. The Centre has been their alternative womb to home. They have used and needed the protection but rarely shown any signs of venturing beyond it. Leaving us, we have imagined, would simply mean returning full-time to the family fortress. But, without miracles or drama, they have all three been slowly growing up inside the Centre. A term before she left, Fran, via a passing passion for one of the staff, finally made it on the boyfriend scene. Now, thanks to pressure from her regular date, she is out at work. When she left, Lizzie, free at last of the bitter jealousy battles with her sister, began to lose her baby image. Her toughness showed itself and she became a tyrannical chairman in Centre meetings. Paul may decide to join the Army when he leaves, not the 'cure' for his fear of violence we would have chosen perhaps, but twice a week he goes to Cadet Corps and even sacrificed a Centre holiday to go abroad with his unit. A short while ago Ange witnessed a sight we never thought we'd see: Paul stopped a fight between two younger boys, gave them a sermon on their stupidity and made them shake hands.

These are no miracles, no brilliant social work salvations. What we can offer, at best, is the right chance, the space and the time, to grow up to be survivors. Negative as it sounds, it may be enough. How many of our kids might otherwise have gone through court to be given the help they needed is impossible for us to guess. Given the chronic lack of provision of any kind and the slowness of legal and social work reaction to non-attendance, most of them would inevitably have been left in their homes or on the streets; at home with little chance of growing beyond the limits of their family life; on the streets with crime as their only outlet and the high risk of Community Home, Borstal and a pattern of life imposed upon them without ever tasting the right of choice. For some of the kids the

Centre came too late anyway. With our help, Sam broke free, physically, from his broken alcoholic mother but now it makes little difference. He's well on his way to total drug addiction. He still trusts us and comes to the Centre for help, but there is little we can do. What he needs should have been given to him ten years ago when a far-sighted report writer predicted this pathetic situation. Others, like Tony and A.J., still in trouble with the law, may take some years to straighten out their lives and even then only if prison hasn't destroyed them first.

Even if, in fifteen years, we were to find only a handful of the Centre kids who had grown up to be happy, it would still have been worth giving one chance to grow to kids who expected no chance at all.

That would be a touching note to end on, a nice little story about sixteen poor deprived kids and a few people who cared. Except that there aren't sixteen kids. There are thousands.

Leaving . . .

It is not very easy for one to put down in words, how you can describe experiences exactly, how you feel about it inside of you. So I think I will tell you about some of the things we done as a group. There are a lot of good and bad things. Looking back now, I think I liked quite a lot of things — like horse riding and looking at interesting things. And what about in the Centre itself? We had quite interesting lessons if you yourself makes them interesting, or maybe that particular subject did not interest you. I can not write down all the things we done, but I hope you will get the meaning of things. In this situation, being with such a small group, you are bound to get close to the kids and teachers. I think that was half the reason it was difficult for me in one way and for them as well, because you can't help liking and having feelings concerned about the people you see quite a lot of. Well leaving for me was not frightening, but I suppose you are frightened in one way. I felt a lot about this which made me depressed thinking about it. Maybe they could see this too, they would try to help as best as they could, but you yourself had to help too, because it don't matter how close you are to someone you have got to have the willpower inside of you. It's there for the taking. I remember talking to one of the teachers when I was depressed about the whole thing . . . . Someone can just talk to me and think I'm not taking a blind bit of notice but with me I learn deep down inside myself.

Now I have left I can't see really what all the fuss was about.

Maybe if I could have seen that it would work out job wise . . .? well that's how it goes. I know now I have left and am not part of the group I see the Centre in a different way. Maybe that's for the good. It does not matter, but at this stage if I was to go back I would be out of place. Feeling different towards them. It's like being left in a room for a long time and then being let out, but when you have got to go back it's like being in a different room again.

Jane

12 A change of view

In July 1974 I left — or to be more precise, I removed my body from the Centre. If I'd been able to remove my mind as well, I probably wouldn't have needed to go through the exorcising agony of writing this book. The fact that I left completely according to a long-arranged plan didn't make it any easier. Before we started the Centre, I'd seen enough of projects that had lived and died through being the total creation of their founders. I didn't want to kill our project by moulding it so completely around ourselves that no one else could ever run it. There was plenty of evidence that this wasn't happening anyway, but even without that risk, I had other, more practical reasons for wanting to leave. I was tired, dried up. I believed in the Centre more than I had ever done but three years of breathing life into it, living it, sleeping it, loving and hating it had exhausted my capacity to fulfil my belief. I could see the danger signs: situations arose and I found myself fighting to control the desire to say, 'We've tried it before, it doesn't work. Take my word for it.' If the place was to keep growing, no one should feel that they had to take anyone's 'word for it'. No situation is ever quite the same: what had failed before might work a second time. Once you begin to see each present picture in terms of the past, it's time to get out, to shake up your certainty, renew your vision. Inevitably, I had become myopic. I could see nothing but the Centre. Scared as I was of re-entry into the world outside, more frightened, perhaps, than any of the kids who left, I knew it was the right time to go.

The kids were not unduly worried at my leaving. Much as I secretly wanted them to sob and plead with me to stay, I felt my conscience relieved of a mighty burden. They didn't need me. When crises arose, I shut myself in the office and let Pete Gurney play at being father. In meetings, I kept quiet. The kids began to look elsewhere for the final word. They had Pete, they still had Ange: the withdrawal was smooth and undramatic. Appropriately enough, A.J. and I left together. Neither of us were necessary any more.

The Centre 1980, by Peter Gurney

Those features which made the Centre a good place in Rob's time are still its main strengths and attractions for those who come now. What we have in 1980, though, is a chance to see the earlier years in some kind of perspective.

By the time Rob did leave in 1973 the Centre had settled down, the kids were becoming a strong, confident group. Looking back, Rob had been pushed into the role of father, the last word in the eyes of the Centre kids. His leaving emphasised the growing need for a different way of working, where decisions and responsibility were shared far more in the whole group. Without Rob the Centre changed in a natural way, each individual having to accept greater responsibility for themselves and others, to see that they could only help themselves by joining in and cooperating as a group, relying on discussion and agreement to go forward. At our meetings we decided how to spend our money, where to go on holiday, what to do about bullying, a theft, what we were to teach. For some of the kids, those who were not ready to see the old and easier ways of doing things go, this change provided, of course, a brilliant opportunity to try it on, to dominate completely. But for all of us it was a demanding, challenging period in which we were forced to look at our positions in the group, the way in which we could best work within it.

Nowadays the structure functions relatively smoothly, is almost taken for granted as it filters through to each new generation of kids. Newcomers see existing rules, sharing, discussion and agreement as the accepted norms and usually quickly understand it as a fair and practical way of getting on together, how it all works to everyone's advantage. The older kids who have been with us a number of years play a crucial role in this. They are seen to be happy joining in, to be doing well, getting plenty back out of the centre. In many ways it is they, more powerfully than the staff, who are able to point the way for the younger ones' futures.

The Centre has now reached that stage where children, when they join, can feel secure and become confident very rapidly. This greater confidence and independence has meant that they have become far more outward looking, wanting to get to know and use places outside the Centre such as colleges, advice services, sports facilities, the law centre, craft workshops — aspects of the community which they need to understand and feel able to use if they are to get on. Less energy and time spent organising ourselves as a group that can work together has meant also that there is more time to devote to our education programme. It remains, of course, geared to the interests and needs of the children who come. Certain things do not change. Shopping for and cooking lunch is as popular as ever, lessons on the supernatural are always in demand, and as in 1972 Centre kids are still finding their way back from the centre of London with just a map and 30p in their pocket.

But the fact that children are here for a longer time has meant that we have needed to present a much more coherent, better organised curriculum. The results so far can be most clearly seen in maths and English. Nowadays the Centre's literacy programme is based on efficient, coordinated small group teaching, covering a range from pre-reading skills to 'O' level English. Yet how far can you extend this approach? How can you best balance the need to remain spontaneous and flexible with the demands of efficient, systematised teaching, which might, in fact, limit the areas of learning which the Centre can offer?

The development of our learning programme has corresponded with the decisions made in 1976 to take pupils only from the 2nd and 1st years. This policy change has produced probably the most important shift in emphasis of the Centre's work. Younger pupils now arrive feeling less let down and frustrated, more open to accept a new start. More crucially, having made sufficient progress at an earlier stage, they are free by their 4th year to concentrate on getting ready to move into the working world, to think about job prospects and to go outside the centre to get experiences and skills which we cannot cover. At the same time they can put into practice what they have already learnt, to test themselves in more demanding settings, yet while still being supported by the Centre.

The result of this has been the development of a leavers' programme designed for our pupils in their final two years. 4th years link into outside options such as child development, typing, plumbing, weightlifting; in their last year they extend this to include courses run at colleges and work experience with local firms. This leavers' course has had a tremendous impact throughout the group, particularly on how the younger ones want to use their time spent with us. It provides a real sense of purpose for them, a realistic target for work done in the first years. They see the 4th and 5th years surviving new challenges, gaining qualifications, starting work and so expect and feel confident that they can and will do the same. In this case then, nothing can succeed like others' success.

The Centre demonstrates ways in which you can work successfully with school non-attenders, an approach which has relevance for the whole school system. It does not only fail those who vote with their feet. But attempts by Local Education Authorities to adopt these methods as a means of working with 'disruptive' pupils have met only limited success. Through its Disruptive Programme of 1978 the ILEA has opened offsite units for pupils whose behaviour had become unacceptable to the schools. These centres have mirrored certain aspects of the alternative education model such as the small group setting, a less formal atmosphere, a better teacher-pupil ratio, a more flexible timetable. They have not reflected, however, the most fundamental features: democratic organisation within the whole group and staff team, cooperative learning and group responsibility, an educational programme geared to the needs of children whose futures lie in their own community. The main reason for this is that the success of the alternative education projects has followed from the autonomy they enjoy. Places like the Centre have been successful because they have had the right to decide on policy matters such as group structure, the learning programme, work done with parents, as well as on key issues like pupil selection, staff appointments, the project's finances. Control in areas such as these has been crucial to us in exploring different approaches and methods of working. Without a similar degree of autonomy, the Disruptive Units are effectively prevented from developing genuinely alternative forms of education. As a consequence they have little chance of being anything more than an exercise in control, primarily serving the immediate interests of individual schools, a means simply of containing pupils whose behaviour the schools consider intolerable or threatening.

Attempts in recent years within the alternative education movement to organise and promote its knowledge and expertise have faltered; often projects have been under too much pressure simply struggling to survive. In December 1979, as part of its programme of cuts, Islington Social Services Committee decided not to renew its annual grant to the Centre. By saving the borough just £4,500, they also stopped another £13,000 of central government funds coming to us. The justification was that truancy is strictly a matter for the schools to handle.

In the end, the issue is not a question of who is responsible for the education and welfare of ordinary children in Islington. The fact is that projects like the Centre, by virtue of their relative autonomy in the voluntary sector, have been able to go beyond conventional views and approaches, to combine skills and methods of different disciplines in exploring new ways of working productively with young people; in so doing they have been able to point to some of the answers, the nature and kinds of change needed in education and care for adolescents. It is on this basis that projects such as the Centre need to be supported.

Throughout the last few months nearly all our energy has been spent fighting the Council's decision. For the younger ones especially this crisis has underlined just how fragile and vulnerable they can feel. Many for a while retreated into hopeless acceptance of the possibility that the Centre would close. But in our campaign to stay open Centre kids who left years ago have given us probably the most encouragement. They have visited the Centre, phoned up, written letters of support. Doreen, who left 3 years ago, wrote a letter to the Council and this is part of it.

'. . . so you see, all the chances I had and needed are going to be needed for kids in the position I was in, and I'd like to see them get that chance. In my opinion the centre is very important and very well needed. It would be a terrible shame to close it. It's not very much in cost to run and the money really goes to good use. I hope very much this letter helps to make you think again and change your mind. I've tried to explain the best way I can, although I could go on writing for ages, because it means a lot to me to see the centre stay open, and I'm sure it means a lot to the kids that are there at the moment.'

(The address of the Centre is: Cromartie House, 41 Tollington Park, London N4, telephone 01-263 0515.)

For those of us who formed the original team — Pete Davis, Alex, Dougal, Ange and myself — leaving enforced a painful change of perspective. Whilst we worked in the Centre we could observe and judge the rest of the world from the safety of that island of sanity. However bizarre the Centre's life may have looked to the outsider, we knew that everything that happened could be understood in terms of the minds and feelings of known individuals. The publicity given to the Centre over its first three years helped to boost our fantasy that it was the best alternative education unit in the country. It was obvious enough that we had been roped into the media circus more for reasons of convenience than because we were manifestly brilliant. A newspaper article brought local radio which in turn caught the attention of television researchers, and appearance on television secured us a place on the media men's list of instant experts. Nevertheless, it was a position worth using to preach what we so passionately believed about education. The cynical, depressing nature of the whole business of being performing monkeys was made bearable by knowing that what we said was based on something alive and honest.

Now, from several years' distance, the Centre appears for what, in cold blood, it really is: just another tiny fringe venture, isolated and struggling for survival, only visible because it serves as a novelty distraction from the vast unchanging mass of educational provision. I am obliged, therefore, to find reasons for having gone through the toil of writing this book, better reasons than exorcising my past, or the pleasure of recording the history of a project that worked, a place where people, for a time, became happier. Twenty people enjoy the Centre. But so what? If it's just an expensive escape route for a small collection of child and adult misfits, then I have no business to sermonise on its virtues. Clearly, I don't believe that it is. I will try to argue that there are very good unemotional reasons why the Centre, and places like it, should exist, but that ultimately there are even better long-term reasons why they shouldn't.

This last step in the argument is the most dangerous. Attempting, as I must, to assess the Centre's validity in the wider context of our school and welfare system, I have no choice but to generalise and thus lay myself open to attack from all sides. Teachers may complain that I am exaggerating the crisis and dismissing as irrelevant years of dedication and effort. Educational researchers may point, quite fairly, to the dearth of factual data in my criticisms. But attacks of that kind have missed the point. I'm not trying to belittle the teaching profession or the importance of researched evidence. My main point is not that teaching or research skills are lacking but that these skills have been too often applied to a crucially distorted vision of educational problems, and therefore wasted. In the struggle to explain truancy, classroom chaos and falling academic standards, much importance has been attached to home and social background as key factors in the problem. Relatively little attention has been given to analysis of the schools themselves, how far differences in school structures and teacher-pupil relationships may be vital determining factors. Eventually, I believe answers will have to be found *inside* the school. Concentration on the development of specialist off-site facilities for the various categories of normal school rejects may only serve, in the long term, to distract attention from the causes of educational breakdown that lie within the schools.

I cannot, however, judge the Centre solely on the basis of its possible long-term impact — whether it delays or hastens the day of reckoning. Educational and social work policymakers are not interested in hypothetical judgement days, and nor are the kids at this moment in search of a relevant education. Had we been concerned at the outset with the long-range implications of setting up the Centre we would probably never have begun. So the immediate questions must be answered. Does it provide effective education and care? Can it improve the life-chances of its pupils at a cost local authorities would be prepared to meet?

I have already implied in earlier chapters that there can be no rigorously objective answers to these questions, but not because we want to take refuge from the scientific eye by talking vaguely about the Unknowability of the Human Soul. It is simply that the Centre's work has not, to date, been the subject of careful research. Only a detailed long-term study of the careers of Centre kids compared with those of a selected control group could begin to suggest definitive answers. And we would be fools not to welcome such a study. There is nothing to be gained by rejecting research on the grounds that its results can and frequently are abused to support political dogmas of widely differing kinds. Research is a powerful weapon and should be used. For the moment, however, we have only our personal judgements to offer — personal but not, we trust, uncritical.

Effective education and care. Effective compared with what? For the majority of the Centre kids the answer, at the time of their referral to the Centre, would have to be: compared with nothing. In most cases the Centre was not chosen as the most suitable provision from a range of available other resources. The realistic alternative to acceptance by the Centre would have been no action at all — or rather no action until continuing truancy or escalating delinquency forced the courts and welfare agencies to provide some other 'solution'. Thus we cannot say with any certainty what would have happened to the Centre kids had they not come to us.

For some — those whose truancy times were spent on the streets rather than in the home — criminal involvement, and the chances of being caught would have continued to rise until the courts made the choice: reception into Care, detention centre, Community Home. Statistics are hardly encouraging. The reconviction rates of children who have been through detention centre and 'Approved School' (as it used to be called) are depressingly high. We have no reason to suppose that such residential provision would have made any of our kids less likely to return to crime on release or any better adjusted to the life-circumstances which led them into crime in the first place. We cannot present the Centre as a miracle cure for young offenders. None of the kids with previous criminal records who came to the Centre gave up crime altogether. What we can say is that attendance at the Centre reduced the opportunity for crime. We would claim, but could not prove, more: that being repeatedly faced with the destructive, unromantic realities of law breaking may have curtailed the criminal careers of several of the Centre kids. The social consequences of stealing within the Centre were difficult to ignore, the fantasy of the underworld hero hard to sustain when the kids could see how pathetically often their friends were caught. While other kids around them were bundled off into residential institutions and away from such direct experience before they had any chance to learn from it, the Centre kids were allowed a breathing space, time to watch, experiment and learn from themselves. Some apparently learnt in their time with us. Others, like A.J., seemed doomed only to provide a lesson in what not to do. All at least had the opportunity to continue the dialogue between themselves and their environment, the chance of learning to survive within it. An opportunity which we believe for most kids is more likely to produce survivors than time spent adjusting to a residential setting which, however good, cannot present the elements of the world to which the kids must return.

For others of the Centre kids the alternative to joining us would have been a different kind of nothing — the nothing of staying at home. It is easy to be arrogant: to claim that remaining locked within a well-worn pattern of family relationships could only have served to stunt growth, deepen depression. But it is dangerous to under-estimate how much the kids gained from their families or to assume that in time they would not have recognised for themselves what their families could not give. Several of the Centre kids who seemed to us so unhealthily bound to home might well in due course have broken free for themselves. For a few it might have been better if they had not had to suffer the confusion of divided loyalties between home and Centre, if instead, they had faced their feelings about home as something wholly within themselves. On balance, however, we believe that there were more kids for whom the break from home restrictions would have come as an explosion of resentment which might have thrown them into totally unexplored territories — areas of experience against which they had no defences. The first mistake could put an end to learning and mark the start of a lifetime of sterile dependency on social work support. Here again if the Centre did nothing more for these kids than keep the dialogue open — a dialogue between self and family conducted at a pace slow enough for experience to be absorbed and learnt from — then their chances of future survival can only have been increased.

The speculation must end there. A comparison between some help and no help is no comparison at all. If we had been offering a clearly defined service to a defined group of kids; if selection had been made on the basis of a clear understanding of each kid's needs; if the choice of the Centre had been from a comprehensive range of facilities: then the analysis of our performance could be much more precise and helpful. As it was, and is, there is no comprehensive set of choices. Many of the kids we accepted should, ideally, never have come to us. What we gave them was a lamentable second best to the non-existent provision they needed.

Yet if, in the short term, we want to prove our case for the continued funding of the Centre, we cannot describe it as second best or better than nothing. The justification must be that it provides a cheaper and more effective method of giving help to truants than the few other facilities that exist. In 1974/5 the cost of running the Centre amounted to a little over £16 000 just over £1000 per child. Over that same period the cost of a place in Care in the London area amounted to around £2500, for an 'Approved School' place to £5000 plus, and the average cost per child in ordinary secondary school to about £1200. Of the sixteen kids attending the Centre at any one time it would be reasonable to assume that three or four might otherwise be in Care and another two or three in 'Approved School'. There is therefore little doubt that the Centre represents a cheap alternative — even to normal school. Whether or not Centre kids will, in their post-school lives, make fewer demands on social resources than they would have done if other provision had been made for them, remains to be seen. We can only assert that we believe they will.

Having stated our claim for survival, we are left with a massive contradiction. If we win this short-term battle we will be in grave danger of contributing to our own defeat in the longer-term fight for recognition of the basic problems. We don't want to be seen as a cheap method of containing the truancy problem, as the basis for yet another specialism in the growing deprivation industry. The implication of that short-term victory would be that the Centre's methods and philosophy are appropriate only for the tiny minority of school misfits; that there is little wrong with our present school system as an education for most normal children. That view is one we totally reject.

To make any generalisations about a whole school system involves the grave risk of sounding naive, of making grossly simplified judgements. Before I go any further I must make clear what I am *not* trying to suggest. I am not trying to say that truants are merely hapless victims of their intolerant schools, with no serious personal problems other than the fact that schools refuse to meet their reasonable demands for help. Nor am I presenting a picture of truants as the courageous few who dare to express the total dissatisfaction with what school offers which all children feel but, for the most part, suppress. My criticisms do not depend, either, on the assumption that all our schools are ineffective, chaotic, on the verge of collapse. And lastly, I am not claiming that radical reform of our school system would miraculously solve the whole range of our social ills.

Compulsory school attendance is a fact of our society, so familiar that most of us rarely step back to recognise its peculiarity. Yet the only other compulsory institution we have is prison. No one asks why prisoners should wish to remain behind bars — the question of motivation is simply irrelevant. All too easily we make the same assumption about school attendance, accept compulsion as a substitute for motivation, and fail to make the crucial inquiry: Why do children go to school? If we allow ourselves an honest answer to that question then the behaviour of the small minority who refuse school will seem very much less extraordinary.

In the Primary years adult pressure is enough. For most children the norm of school attendance is merely a fixed feature of their lives. But beyond that, from eleven to sixteen, why do they stay? Escape is easy enough; the legal penalties are not fearsome or immediate. Those well-known statistics on educational achievement convey part of the answer. For middle-class parents, anxious that their offspring should maintain their status, for ambitious parents who want their children 'to better themselves', school is vitally important. These children recognise its potential for themselves. Belief in the payoff provides its own compulsion. But for the army of 'also rans', who know at the age of eleven what the educational statisticians tell us, that there will be no payoff in material terms, we must look elsewhere for motive. There must be several answers.

However little their parents may believe in school as useful for their children, there is, firstly, the fact of law. Few parents will want to run the risk of court if there is nothing to be gained by it. Fathers who make their living out of thieving may still refuse quite logically to let their kids 'bunk off' school — it's a 'mug's game'. Not only is the likelihood of being caught for it great, the kids also risk getting involved in amateur crime, and getting caught for that too. Having the kids in school has one major negative advantage: it keeps them 'out of trouble'. And for a minority of working-class parents there is still the hope that school may do more than that: there is the dream that they may get lucky, the kids might make it.

Pressure from parents will get the majority to school and being there together must provide the main reason for wanting to stay. For most of the kids the principal enjoyment cannot be a profound enthusiasm for what the teachers try to give them — neither they nor their parents believe lessons contain much that could be relevant or useful to them. The pleasure must come from 'being with their mates', being in with the gangs in the playground, joining in the teacher-baiting games during lessons, feeling the solidarity of being part of 'us' against 'them'. Out of school they will probably be alone and vulnerable to attack. 'Them' won't be the teachers who can be teased and ignored with relative impunity, 'them' will be the police with the power to inflict real punishment. Being inside with friends is generally preferable, even though it means putting up with the tedium of lessons and petty regulations, to the loneliness, boewsom and risks of playing truant.

But being bored with most lessons is not the same thing as having no curiosity, interest or desire to learn. Behind the apathy and disruption, the kids still want to learn. In an otherwise dreary week's timetable there may be one or two lessons they can see some point to, that they actually enjoy. Trapped into having to appear to be in school and 'out of trouble', kids may still have enough freedom to make their own individual compromises: they may choose to suffer through the week until Wednesday's art lesson then get their mark and disappear on the remaining days; morning school may be tolerated for the sake of the afternoon's carpentry class; lessons they hate can be spent in the toilets. The various games for making attendance bearable can be played successfully. The kids who play them never appear on the truancy statistics. They can avoid their parents, their teachers, avoid notice altogether.

Seen in this way, rigid distinctions between the 'normal' kids who attend school and the 'abnormal' kids who don't, begin to disappear. There is no single major motive force driving most kids to attend which is patently absent in kids who play truant. It is much more a question of delicate balances. Active pressure from parents to attend may be lacking but their kids may still go — to be with their friends. But if there is positive parental pressure against attendance then there is real reason to stay at home. A mother who needs support to face her drunken husband or the depressing burden of her younger children can be reason enough: the family is a real and accepted part of life; school is not. Days at home with mum develop their own routine and rewards: being needed, treated like an adult, having power over younger brothers and sisters. The longer the kids stay away from school, the less reason there will be for ever going back. Other truants and the mother's friends, will replace mates in school. Non-attenders at home may, like Rita or Sue, become dragged down by family problems, bored and depressed, but returning to school will seem no solution. It will be substituting one form of frustrating boredom which has, at least, some security and rewards for another which has lost what little pleasure it had.

There will be just as good a reason for absence if, as for Fran, Paul, Mike and Jamie, school life offers more pain than pleasure. What they have to face is a pupil society which is tough and frequently vicious. Timid and unsure kids will have little chance of survival. Support and protection from teachers will rarely be enough. If these kids cannot quickly find their own clique in school, they can become isolated and scapegoated, and given every reason to take the risk of truancy to escape the pressure. Once they have found, like Jamie, a gentler world to live in, school can only become progressively more awful a prospect. The safety of being alone or with friends who won't dominate or bully makes pressure of any kind more difficult to face. The dream of being tough, being 'one of the lads' remains. Knowing that they're not eats away the remnants of self-confidence.

It's tempting to simplify the complicated pattern of pressures into a few neat generalisations: to assume, for instance, that social success can compensate totally for academic failure or that academic success can immunise kids to the values of their peers. Neither statement can be accepted. The knowledge that they are destined to leave school as academic failures does not give kids any guaranteed escape from the humiliation of that failure. However much they may insist to them-selves and to one another that school values are meaningless, the awful fact remains that they must live each day in an institution based on standards which label them losers. The more desperate they are for recognition and approval, the worse that humiliation becomes. Better then to be a gang leader outside the school where those standards do not apply, than to face the contradiction of being the Remedial Stream hero. Yet the contradictions can be as painful in the A stream for the kids who have broken those mysterious codes of learning. Tony, for instance, possessed all the necessary skills to reach university, and the beginning of genuine enthusiasm. But to pursue that aim would have required a sacrifice he could not make — the loss of his friends, of earning power, of status. Compared to these things school was alien and unreal. He sacrificed school to resolve the contradiction.

Of course, the state of education in the country as a whole is not as I have described. What I have presented is just not credible. In rural areas and in most small towns truancy is an insignificant problem. The children attend, the teachers teach in relative calm. If the children leave without qualifications they have at least gained something — friends, the skills of social survival. There are few signs of crisis, it seems. It is in the depressed urban areas that crisis point has been reached. I am saying nothing new. The inner city problems have been recognised for years. The poverty, depression, rotten housing, social breakdown have been researched to exhaustion, money and resources poured in in increasing quantities. If schools in these areas are demoralised, chaotic and ineffective there can be no surprise about the fact. They are merely reaping the harvest of the surrounding social disaster. Education authorities can claim to have tried hard, giving extra resources to the schools, additional salary incentives to the teachers, developing a whole science of compensatory education. If there is little evidence of dramatic success, it may easily be argued that final remedies must be found elsewhere.

Certainly the remedy for our social ills cannot be the sole responsibility of our school system. But if we look at potential influences on our children we see that school lays claim to thirty hours a week of every child's life. Of our social institutions only television takes as much. Yet, compared to television, school, despite all the expenditure and dedication, has for many children only a marginal impact. Michael Power, researching into schools in East London, compared rates of truancy and delinquency in apparently similar schools with apparently similar catchment areas and found sizeable variations in the factors measured. The only available explanation was that some unidentified feature in the schools themselves produced those differences.

And that is where I believe the search for answers must begin — in the schools themselves. We must ask the most basic, unsophisticated questions which have been largely ignored. Because school is compulsory, because the reason for attendance amongst those destined for academic success is obvious, we have chosen to take for granted the most fundamental prerequisite for all learning — the desire to learn. What we will find if we examine our crisis schools in the light of that principle is: too many teachers who have lost faith in the relevance of what they teach, too many children with no belief in the relevance of what they are being asked to learn, and a school structure which is making it increasingly difficult for the two sides to find any meeting place for the regeneration of faith in learning.

Evidently the existence of the large comprehensive does not, in itself, make the creation of good schools impossible. If it did, then there would not be those marked differences between apparently similar schools. A head teacher with faith in his vision of the school can still gather a team of like-minded teachers around him and breath life into the whole structure. But the odds are not on his side. All too easily the standardised large comprehensive system serves merely to accelerate the downward spiral. The system itself can begin to dictate the life of the school. In schools of a thousand pupils and over eighty staff, personal contact becomes very hard to achieve. The problems of controlling large numbers means that there is constant pressure towards regimented, formal kinds of contact, which inevitably tend to be impersonal and alienating for staff and kids alike. The more impersonal the contact the more likely it will be that teacher-pupil relationships will degenerate into a state of warfare: teachers fighting merely to control rather than teach kids fighting to assert the values of their own social structure against those of a school structure which seems to deny them any recognition. The main casualty is basic respect between staff and pupils. The kids come to despise the teachers for their loss of control, for their lack of conviction in what they teach. The teachers begin to despise their pupils' society which seems so brutalised and destructive. No amount of educational hardware can compensate for that loss of respect, because it is a basic prerequisite for the whole learning process.

There are no easy answers. If tomorrow an edict released all over schools into free democratic bargaining the result would probably be utter chaos. Neither side, staff or pupils, would have any agreed demands to bring to the conference table. A survey of the pronouncements of the major teaching unions would not reveal a coherent set of educational priorities. Most kids, when questioned, have little idea of what they want to learn. It is not depressing; it is merely the inevitable product of the fact that, for so long, there has been no real discussion among those directly involved in education about their own educational needs.

So where should we begin? The teachers would do well to begin with themselves. It is time, surely, for the teaching unions to divert their attention from the symptoms of the disorder — classroom chaos, playground violence, high staff turnover — to the simple fact that they cannot teach in schools as they are, and to examine the structure of those schools. They might analyse how little time they have for basic discussion of school policies, how difficult it is to influence those policies, how little support they can give each other in their classrooms, how often it happens that the various subject departments are in conflict with one another for time and resources. If teachers see it as important to understand the world in which their pupils live, how much more difficult is this made by having to live themselves distant from their teaching area? If their pupils find much of the written teaching material irrelevant, should not more time and equipment be available to allow schools to generate more of their own locally-based material? If, school by school, staffs could reach a state where they worked as a unified body with agreed educational principles on which their schools were moulded, they would face their pupils from a position of strength. The rebirth of mutual respect could begin.

At a national level policy makers conduct games of educational dogma which affect the lives of millions of children. Yet pleas for careful educational experiment at a local level are usually met with blind refusal: we must not turn our children into guinea-pigs. It is too late. They already are, on a massive scale. Yet we know well enough what the alternative to radical experiment is. It is that process which allowed the Centre to exist; a process by which more and more children whose needs are not met within the main school system are labelled deviant and are isolated into categories of disturbance. It won't work. Schools will never be able to shrink the boundaries of the 'normal' enough to solve the problem that lies inside the school itself.

No one who worked in the Centre would pretend to hold the grand design for the new education system. The Centre is an attempt to look for answers, for ourselves and for the kids, and this book is an attempt to show where the answers might be. What worries us finally is not the fate of our kids. We believe that the kids still have the strength to be honest about their problems. We doubt that our education authorities can finally share that honesty.

Bibliography

This is not an attempt to provide a definitive reading list. I have simply noted a few books which I feel may be useful for readers sufficiently irritated or stimulated to pursue some of the educational issues that I hope I have raised.

For a background to the arguments of the 'deschoolers'
Holt, J., *How children fail*, Penguin, 1971
Illich, I., *Deschooling society*, Penguin, 1969
Neill, A. S., *Summerhill: a radical approach to education*, Gollancz, 1962

For very different views of truancy
Kahn, J. H. and Nursten, J. P., *Unwillingly to school*, Pergamon Press, 1968
Tyerman, M., *Truancy*, University of London Press, 1968

For attempts to examine, in a variety of ways, what happens inside our schools, and what basic assumptions underlie our educational system
Bronfenbrenner, U., *Two worlds of childhood, USA and USSR*, Allen and Unwin, 1972
Corrigan, P. D., *Examination of the life of the classroom* (unpublished Ph.D. thesis, University of Durham)
Ford Safari Project: Innovation, evaluation, research and the problem of control, University of East Anglia
Ford Teaching Project, University of East Anglia
Hargreaves, D., *Social relations in a secondary school*, Routledge & Kegan Paul, 1970
McKenzie, R. F., *State school*, Penguin, 1970

Lastly, for the views of other alternative education projects
Dennison, G., *Lives of Children*, Penguin
The Reports of the White Lion Free School (obtainable from 57 White Lion Street, London N1
The Reports of the Bethnal Green Intermediate Education Centre (obtainable from IEC, St John's Crypt, Roman Road, London E2